FROST ON TH[E...]

A Play in Three Acts for W[...]

By

T. B. MORRIS

LONDON
SAMUEL FRENCH LIMITED

Copyright © 1951 by Samuel French Ltd
All Rights Reserved

FROST ON THE ROSE is fully protected under the copyright laws of the British Commonwealth, including Canada, the United States of America, and all other countries of the Copyright Union. All rights, including professional and amateur stage productions, recitation, lecturing, public reading, motion picture, radio broadcasting, television and the rights of translation into foreign languages are strictly reserved.

ISBN 978-0-573-11489-2

www.samuelfrench.co.uk
www.samuelfrench.com

FOR AMATEUR PRODUCTION ENQUIRIES

UNITED KINGDOM AND WORLD EXCLUDING NORTH AMERICA

plays@samuelfrench.co.uk
020 7255 4302/01

Each title is subject to availability from Samuel French, depending upon country of performance.

CAUTION: Professional and amateur producers are hereby warned that FROST ON THE ROSE is subject to a licensing fee. Publication of this play does not imply availability for performance. Both amateurs and professionals considering a production are strongly advised to apply to the appropriate agent before starting rehearsals, advertising, or booking a theatre. A licensing fee must be paid whether the title is presented for charity or gain and whether or not admission is charged.

No one shall make any changes in this title for the purpose of production. No part of this book may be reproduced, stored in a retrieval system, or transmitted in any form, by any means, now known or yet to be invented, including mechanical, electronic, photocopying, recording, videotaping, or otherwise, without the prior written permission of the publisher. No one shall upload this title, or part of this title, to any social media websites.

The right of T.B. Morris to be identified as author of this work has been asserted in accordance with Section 77 of the Copyright, Designs and Patents Act 1988.

For
PAT BELL McKENZIE

CHARACTERS

PRINCESS MARY
PRINCESS ELIZABETH
LADY JANE GREY
MISTRESS ELLEN, attendant on Jane
THE DUCHESS OF SUFFOLK, Jane's Mother
LADY ELEANOR BRANDON, Jane's Aunt
THE DUCHESS OF NORTHUMBERLAND
KATE, a Serving Maid
RICHARD, a Page
1ST WOMAN IN STREET
2ND WOMAN IN STREET
3RD WOMAN IN STREET

Optional characters : A Herald, King Edward VI, an Executioner, an Officer. Townsfolk, Soldiers and Attendants may be added if desired. For suitable doubling, see Production Notes.

SYNOPSIS OF SCENERY
(a simple curtain setting may be employed)

PROLOGUE

ACT I

SCENE 1   A room in the Duke of Suffolk's house at Sheen. A July morning, 1552.

SCENE 2   A London street

SCENE 3   The room in the Duke of Suffolk's house. An afternoon in May, 1553.

ACT II

SCENE 1   A London street.

SCENE 2   The room in the Duke of Suffolk's house. The evening of July 5th, 1553.

SCENE 3   Outside a London tavern.

SCENE 4   The anteroom to Jane Grey's bedchamber in the Tower of London. The afternoon of July 10th, 1553.

SCENE 5   At Framlingham Castle.

SCENE 6   The anteroom in the Tower. The night of July 17th, 1553.

ACT III

SCENE 1   The anteroom in the Tower. The morning of January 25th, 1554.

SCENE 2   Outside the Tower. Just after dawn on February 12th, 1554.

SCENE 3   An upper room in the house of Nathaniel Partridge, on Tower Green. Just before ten o'clock on the same morning.

PRODUCTION NOTES

This play, though dealing with a series of events in which men were active, has been devised for performance by all-women teams, with a cast of twelve women. It has been possible to do this—leaving the men just off stage on the fringe of the story—because women did take a very large part in the happenings described. The three rival claimants of the throne were all women. The Duchess of Suffolk was certainly a stronger character than her husband, and had a great deal to do with the direction of events which led to her unfortunate daughter's execution. The Duchess of Northumberland, also, had a powerful personality.

While, for the sake of stage economy, a few minor liberties have been taken with time and place, the foundations of this play are sound history and the principal scenes (as, for instance, Jane Grey's beating to make her consent to her marriage) are based on fact.

The part of Richard, the page, will present no difficulty to a girl, and slender girls always make most attractive stage boys. The other male parts: Herald, Edward VI, Executioner and Officer, may be doubled from the female characters; the Herald with Richard, Edward VI with Kate, the Executioner and the Officer with 3rd Woman. Or, if preferred, they may be omitted. The stylized Prologue is designed to give the audience an easy grasp of Henry VIII's will regarding the succession, as well as to provide an original introduction and to give Jane Grey an opportunity to make the speech which she actually made from the scaffold, and so heighten the drama of her story. If necessary, however, the Prologue may be omitted. The interlude scenes of women in the street provide contrast (in class and tone) and amply cover what scene changes are necessary.

The play is designed for simple production using a curtain setting on a small stage. Tudor roses and heraldic shields and banners, as well as tapestries and/or painted cloths, will help to decorate the settings. The interludes may be played on the main stage before the front curtain, or on a forestage or small platform to one side. The lighting may be quite simple. On the other hand, settings and lighting may be considerably elaborated where facilities permit, and the cast may be enlarged as desired by the addition of Townsfolk, Soldiers and Attendants.

In a simple production it is intended that the furniture of Act I, Scene 1 shall be used for the following principal scenes (as shown) with the addition only of the chair of state and rostrum. The steps of the rostrum should be used at the window in Act III, Scene 3.

It is suggested that Jane Grey should wear a black and white dress for the Prologue and the end of Act III, Scene 3. For Act I Scenes 1 and 3, Act II Scene 2, and the beginning of Act III Scene 3, she should wear something white with a light pattern to emphasize her youth in contrast with the others. For Act II Scenes 4 and 6, and Act III Scene 1, her dress should be somewhat as described by Kate in Act II Scene 4.

Suitable records of period music will be found in the *Columbia History of Music, Volume I.*

For those who wish to use piano music, simple piano solos (a little later in date but quite suitable) are published in *A Selection from the Fitzwilliam Virginal Book*, published by the British and Continental Music Agencies, Ltd, 125 Shaftesbury Avenue, London W.C.2.

FROST ON THE ROSE

PROLOGUE

Music, which stops as the HERALD *comes on to the forestage before the lowered* CURTAIN. *He carries a scroll.*

HERALD (*addressing the audience*). Good people, of your charity pray for the soul of the most high and mighty Prince, Henry the Eighth, our late Sovereign Lord and King, of blessed memory. (*He pauses.*) Be it known unto all that this is the will of our late Sovereign. (*He reads from the scroll.*) In the name of God, and of the Glorious and Blessed Virgin our Lady Saint Mary, and of all the Holy Company of Heaven, this is the order of our succession. Our son, the Prince Edward.

(EDWARD VI *enters* L. *He is a weakly, pathetic boy of fifteen. He wears a crown and robe of state and carries sceptre and orb. He crosses the forestage and goes off* R.)

If he should die childless, and we should have no children by our beloved wife Katherine, or any other wives that we may have hereafter, he shall be succeeded by our daughter, the Princess Mary.

(PRINCESS MARY *enters* L. *She is a woman of thirty-six, serious, kindly but obstinate, short-sighted and with a deep voice. Her costume always includes a rosary and crucifix. Her movements are slow. She crosses the forestage and goes off* R.)

If she shall have no children, she shall be succeeded by our daughter, the Princess Elizabeth.

(PRINCESS ELIZABETH *enters briskly* L. *She is nineteen, fair-haired, high-spirited, in vivid contrast with her sister. She dances across the forestage and goes off* R.)

If she have no children, the succession shall pass to the Lady Jane Grey.

(LADY JANE GREY *enters* L., *reading a book. She is a girl of sixteen, small, slight, pretty, with fair hair and a prim manner. She wears the black and white dress which she will wear for her execution. She crosses slowly and goes off* R. *After she has gone, the* HERALD *turns* R. *and goes off, still reading.*)

And thereafter to the Lady Katherine Grey and the Lady Mary Grey; and, failing heirs to these . . .

(*The* HERALD'S *voice has faded out. If desired it may be cross-faded with a short burst of riotous music. The* 1ST *and* 2ND WOMEN *enter* L. *of the forestage, gossiping together. They are women of the people, the former sharp and garrulous, the latter slower and stupid.*)

1ST WOMAN. Ay! I can mind it as well as 'twas yesterday. An' so should you if you'd any wits.

2ND WOMAN. What?

1ST WOMAN. Why—King 'Enry's funeral! Great doin's they 'ad. 'Tis said they spent a thousand pound on the drinks.

2ND WOMAN. A thousand pound? They couldn't never drink all that.

1ST WOMAN. Couldn't they? Don't you know men? (*She chuckles.*) But what come of it all? I asks you—what come on't?

2ND WOMAN. A mort o' drunkenness, I should reckon.

1ST WOMAN. Knot-pate! That was cured the day after. I means all the business o' the succession. Lor' love us! Don't you mind it? There were all but another bloody war like the Wars o' the Roses. First there was poor little King Edward . . .

(EDWARD VI, *dressed as before, enters* R. *of the forestage. He is ill and frightened. The* WOMEN *take no notice of him, but appear to gossip.*)

EDWARD (*to the audience; pleading*). Good people—I pray you be good to me. 'Tis an uneasy matter to be a king and to follow such a king as my father. My crown is heavy, and the ceremonies so long—and I am tired and ill. My uncle Somerset, the Lord Protector, made me do lessons and listen to long, long sermons. He'd never let me play like other boys. (*Momentarily brightening.*) My uncle Sudeley was better. He used to amuse me and give me money. He was the right sort of uncle for a boy— (*sadly*) but they cut off his head. And now they've cut off uncle Somerset's head, too, and Northumberland has taken his place. I'm afraid of him— (*he retreats a little*) and there are shadows. (*He glances about fearfully.*) Good people—be good to me. (*He goes off wearily* L., *or through the curtains* C.)

1ST WOMAN. Of course, he didn't last long. Never had a chance. And I don't know as Queen Mary's much happier . . .

(*She continues to mime conversation.* MARY *enters* R., *holding her crucifix in her hands.*)

MARY (*to the audience*). My mother—God rest her—was a great Princess of Aragon, and greater than her many troubles. My father —may God forgive him—treated her shamefully. I was a child when they took her from me, and I never saw her again. (*She pauses thoughtfully, and then braces herself to continue.*) Now I have but hardly come to mine own—yet what I have I will rule. (*Sincerely.*) It is my wish to love you, my people, and that I may have your love— (*proudly*) but I will establish again the true Church, and abolish heresy—even, if need be, by blood and fire.

(ELIZABETH *dances on* R., *laughing, and catches* MARY *by the arm.*)

ELIZABETH (*laughing*). Sister, sister! Heavy hand makes poor pastry, and who loves a long face? *I* could show you how to win their hearts—ay, and how to rule them—though *my* mother was no Princess of Spain.

MARY (*stiffly*). Nor princess of anywhere. Have care, Elizabeth! I love you, but do not go too far.

ELIZABETH (*laughing*). Oh, I shall never wear the crown, but, by m' faith, I shall continue to wear my head. Marry an Englishman, sister, and get an English prince. Stop thinking your Spanish thoughts.

MARY (*turning away towards* L.). I would have love and honesty, but there is hate and double-dealing—plotting . . . (*She moves towards* L.) You, Elizabeth, speak one thing and plot another.

ELIZABETH (*darting after her*). Mary! On my soul, I protest . . .

(*She checks and stands staring at* MARY, *momentarily serious.*)

MARY (*pausing, her back to* ELIZABETH). I said, have a care, sister. (*Sadly.*) Bethink you of that poor, misguided child, Jane Grey.

(*She goes off* L. ELIZABETH, *sobered, looks after her, then glances* R., *shivering. For a moment she pauses, then follows* MARY *quietly off* L. *A funeral bell begins to toll.*)

1ST WOMAN. Lady Jane Grey . . . Poor little soul! But nine days Queen—and she had no will to it, they say. 'Twas her parents forced her into it—especially her mother—and then deserted her.

2ND WOMAN. She's young to die.

1ST WOMAN. Ay—but sixteen. Like a rosebud caught by early frost.

(JANE *enters* R., *walking solemnly and carrying a prayer-book. She is followed by the* EXECUTIONER, *who is dressed in red, with a red mask, and carries a great axe with its edge towards her. He is as big as possible, towering over her.* JANE, *with the* EXECUTIONER *standing behind her, addresses the audience.*)

JANE. Good people, I am come here to die. (*She pauses briefly.*) My offence against the Queen's Highness was only in consenting to the device of others, which is now termed treason—but it was never of my seeking, who knew little of the law and less of the title to the crown. I do wash my hands thereof in innocence before God and in the face of you, good Christian people, this day. I pray you all— to bear me witness that I die a true Christian woman, and that I look to be saved by—the mercy of God, in the merit of the blood of His only son Jesus Christ . . . (*Faltering a little.*) And now, good people, while I am living, I pray you assist me with your prayers.

(*She holds out her hands for a moment, then turns and goes slowly off
L., followed by the* EXECUTIONER. *A roll of drums is heard, together
with the continued tolling of the bell. The* 1ST *and* 2ND WOMEN *go
off, weeping. The sounds of drums and bell fade out. The* HERALD
enters.)

HERALD. That was the prologue and the epilogue. This is the story.

(*He goes off. Gay music of virginals is heard.*)

ACT I
Scene 1

SCENE.—*A room in the Duke of Suffolk's house at Sheen. A July morning*, 1552.

There is an entrance down R., *from the garden, and another up* L. *from the inner rooms. Across the* R. *corner, up stage, is a long window with a window-seat before it. Against the back wall at* R.C., *is a small chest or table, and, to* L. *of this, a cupboard or sideboard. A refectory table is set down* L.C., *at an angle, and has a chair above it and a stool below it.*

(*See the Ground Plan at the end of the Play.*)

When the CURTAIN *rises, the garden is filled with sunshine. On the window-sill, table and chest are vases of roses and other summer flowers. On the cupboard are a large jug of ale and two or three tankards. On the table, looking distinctly out of place, stands a pair of man's riding-boots.* KATE, *a young serving-maid, is down* C. *near the end of the table, against which* RICHARD, *a page, is leaning. She is bending towards him, dramatically making the most of a story which at once scares and thrills her. Her face is close to his.*

KATE (*tensely*). An' you'd been here last night you might ha' seen it.

RICHARD (*amused by her seriousness, with male superiority*). Last night, sweeting, I had an errand for my Lord Duke, which ended, by the grace of God, as near a tavern as makes no matter. (*He chuckles.*)

KATE (*impatiently*). Oh, listen! 'Twas a dreadful thing, and a portent.

(*The music stops.*)

(*Fearfully.*) A skeleton hand with an axe, all dripping blood.

RICHARD. What else should an axe drip?

KATE. Listen, I say! It thrust out from the panelling of the long gallery, as my Lord and my Lady went to bed.

RICHARD. I'll not believe it.

KATE. 'Tis true. The story's everywhere. And strange shapes have been seen—and there are whisperings . . .

RICHARD (*interrupting*). Little knot-pate! You may have your ghosts. What I'll *not* believe is that my Lord and my Lady were *together* on their way to bed. (*He grips her shoulders and draws her closer, grinning, speaking confidentially.*) Had you said my Lady and

Master Adrian Stopes...
KATE (*aghast*). Wickedness!
RICHARD (*laughing*). Lechery!

(*He suddenly kisses* KATE, *taking her by surprise.*)

KATE. Oh!
RICHARD (*holding her as she struggles*). Her Grace of Suffolk and his Grace's groom of the chambers. There's a real tale for you...
KATE. Mercy o' God—hush! And let me go!

(RICHARD *laughs and tries to kiss* KATE *again. She boxes his ears, breaks free, turns, and runs to the door* L. *He chases her. As she is running off, she is stopped by* MRS ELLEN, *a firm but kindly woman of middle age, who, having been nurse to* LADY JANE GREY, *is now her attendant.* ELLEN *grabs* RICHARD. KATE *pauses to enjoy his discomfiture.*)

ELLEN. How often have I told you, Richard, that I'll not have young rampallians making trouble among my maids.
RICHARD. Trouble, Mistress Ellen? I—I came on my lord's order with his boots.
ELLEN (*pushing* RICHARD *down to the table, and pointing*). And left them there to give his Grace no cause for bending.
RICHARD (*affecting surprise*). By m' faith! They must ha' taken wings...

(ELLEN *good-naturedly boxes his ears and releases him.*)

Ow!
ELLEN. Out, young coystril!

(RICHARD *grabs the boots, runs up stage with them and places them* R. *of the cupboard. Then, making a face at* KATE, *he runs past her, and off* L. KATE *makes to slip off after him, but* ELLEN *moves to* C., *turns, and calls her.*)

Kate! Come here.

(KATE *moves towards* ELLEN, *who points to the place on the table where the boots have stood.* KATE *takes a duster from the pocket of her apron and polishes that part of the table. The music of the virginals begins again.*)

KATE (*as she polishes*). 'Twas the bloody axe. I was but telling him, and...
ELLEN (*interrupting*). Axe! (*Easing above the chair.*) Let me hear no more o' such nonsense. Keep your hands and eyes for your work, and— (*she takes* KATE *by the shoulders and swings her round*) mark me, your lips for your prayers. Then, an you pray not as the Papists do, no ghostly visitations can harm you, girl. (*With a grim chuckle.*) 'Tis visitations o' the flesh you've more cause to fear.

KATE (*suddenly glancing* L.). Here's her Grace ...

(ELLEN *releases* KATE *and moves up* R.C. KATE *crosses down* R., *and stands facing* L. *The* DUCHESS OF SUFFOLK *sweeps into the room from* L., *followed by* LADY ELEANOR BRANDON, *her sister.* ELLEN *and* KATE *curtsy.* SUFFOLK *is a woman of middle age, still handsome. A niece of Henry VIII, she has all the bad qualities of the Tudors and none of their greatness. She is boisterous, cruel, inordinately proud, and quite unscrupulous in her pursuit of ambition.* BRANDON *is a few years younger, by no means lacking in strength of character, but at once more cautious and more scrupulous than her sister.* KATE *rises from her curtsy and slips off* R. ELLEN *is about to go off* L. *when* SUFFOLK, *who is* L. *of the chair above the table, stops her.*)

SUFFOLK (*abruptly*). Who is playing the virginals?
ELLEN. The Lady Jane, your Grace, or so I should ...
SUFFOLK (*interrupting, harshly*). It has been forbidden. Go and tell her to stop it on the instant.
BRANDON (*moving below and* L. *of the table ; protesting*). But, Frances, 'tis a harmless thing ...
SUFFOLK (*turning and interrupting*). Enough, sister! *I* choose my daughter's occupations. She neglects her studies for this music.
ELLEN (*boldly*). I have told your Grace before that the Lady Jane studies too hard.
SUFFOLK (*turning to* ELLEN). And who gave you leave, nurse, to form opinions?
ELLEN. My heart, madam. To see the child so pale, more a scholar already than any young girl should ...
SUFFOLK (*interrupting*). Out! Do as I say. (*Significantly.*) I'll speak with my daughter anon. (*Her hands clench suggestively.*) Out, woman!

(ELLEN *makes a stiff little bob and goes coldly off* L.)

BRANDON. Sister—Ellen is right.
SUFFOLK. Ellen presumes upon her position as an old servant. (*She moves round the chair above the table and sits.*) And you, Eleanor, also presume. I will manage my own affairs, I give you thanks.
BRANDON (*coldly*). It might profit you to take advice.
SUFFOLK (*jumping up furiously, thumping the table*). God's blood, I ... (*Trying to control herself, sitting again.*) But we'll not brabble over Jane.

(BRANDON *turns up stage, moves* R. *to the window, and looks off. The music stops.* SUFFOLK *nods with satisfaction.*)

Ah! (*To* BRANDON.) Master Aylmer, her tutor, has complained to me on this matter.

BRANDON (*swinging round; indignantly*). Master Aylmer! All this cramming of Latin, Greek, Hebrew! Dusty hours of books and philosophers; dry tutors with sermons as long as their self-righteous noses! And little Jane not yet fifteen. (*Moving in up* L.C.) I have asked you before, sister—to what end is all this?

SUFFOLK (*stiffening*). To what end? That Jane shall be a shining light in the Reformed Church. In this darkened England we need...

BRANDON (*interrupting; dryly*). Not that old story again, Frances. Not to me. (*Easing down a little.*) You don't believe it yourself.

(SUFFOLK *again starts up angrily and moves a pace towards* BRANDON.)

SUFFOLK. You know my husband is a champion of Reform. Our duty...

BRANDON (*interrupting; with more impatience*). Duty, duty, duty! *Your* duty, Frances, has been ever to yourself. Your children are pawns on your board.

SUFFOLK (*starting*). Pawns? (*Sneering.*) And that from you! Have I not heard that the Duke of Northumberland has been with you of late on a certain errand not unconnected with—a pawn? (*She laughs unpleasantly, turns, and sits again.*)

BRANDON (*calmly*). You have heard half of the matter. The Duke would have married his son Guildford to my daughter Margaret—ay, he would. (*She moves swiftly to* SUFFOLK *and stands over her.*) But have you heard that I sent him packing?

SUFFOLK (*amazed*). You refused the match? Then you are a fool, Eleanor. The King himself approved it.

BRANDON. The King? That poor boy approves what he is told to approve, and Northumberland is his present master. (*She pauses.*) Northumberland aims higher. (*Significantly.*) Nor is he the only one who aims too high.

SUFFOLK. Have you come here, sister, to put me in a choler?

BRANDON. I have come here, sister, to speak of that matter you have broached but now; to warn you...

SUFFOLK. Warn?

BRANDON. To remind you, then, that we are too near the throne for comfort, you and I.

(*She pauses. Their eyes meet for a moment.*)

I will not be embroiled in the struggle for the throne when the King dies. (*She turns and starts to move down* L.)

SUFFOLK. When the King *dies*?

BRANDON (*checking at* L.C.). He's a sickly boy—will last another year at most. And then...! (*She makes an expressive gesture.*) What a coil! That's why I'll ha' none of Northumberland and his lordling. He'll not use me as stepping-stone to his ambition. (*She moves down and gazes into the garden.*)

SUFFOLK (*concerned*). The King will not die. He will grow out of his weakness and ... (*She breaks off, rises abruptly, goes up to the cupboard and pours ale into one of the tankards, takes a hearty drink and wipes her mouth with her hand.*)

BRANDON (*turning and watching her*). And—what *you* will?

(SUFFOLK *laughs.*)

Beware, sister. Your husband is weak.

SUFFOLK. 'Fore God, *I* am not!

BRANDON (*moving to* L.C.). Oh, I doubt not you wear the breeches in this house. But Suffolk is no more than the shadow of Northumberland. Or, shall we say, a jackal who follows a lion?

SUFFOLK. Northumberland a lion? A mangy lion, then. (*As she eases down* C.) He may jet himself now, he and that Duchess of his, but he will soon find that his teeth are rotten. He may have been Warwick before he was Northumberland, but the house of Warwick is not what it was. We, who are of royal blood, may have somewhat to show this upstart Northumberland.

(ELLEN *enters* L. SUFFOLK *turns to her.*)

Well?

ELLEN. The Duchess of Northumberland, madam——

SUFFOLK. What!

ELLEN. —is here to see your Grace.

SUFFOLK (*to* BRANDON; *with an uneasy laugh*). Talk of the devil! (*To* ELLEN.) Bid her come here.

(ELLEN *goes off* L. SUFFOLK *looks at* BRANDON, *who moves quickly to her.*)

BRANDON (*urgently, in a low voice*). Frances—remember what I have said. Content yourself with what you have.

SUFFOLK. Those who do that are like to lose even what they have. I've no chicken's liver. (*Viciously.*) Leave me and my concerns alone. (*She moves up to the cupboard.*)

(BRANDON *turns away and moves to the window, sitting on the seat.* SUFFOLK *takes another great draught from the tankard, sets it down on the cupboard, takes up the boots left by* RICHARD, *carries them down* R. *and throws them contemptuously off through the door. Then she moves up* C. *with a sneering laugh.*)

You may leave by the garden, sister, an you please. (*She gestures towards the door* R.)

BRANDON. No. I'll not be driven out by that woman.

SUFFOLK. As you will.

(ELLEN *enters* L., *and stands above the door.*)

ELLEN. Her Grace the Duchess of Northumberland.

(*The* DUCHESS OF NORTHUMBERLAND *enters* L. *and moves to* L.C. *She is of middle age and still beautiful. Though lower in birth than* SUFFOLK, *she has more poise and self-control, and therefore more of the appearance of a great lady. She, also, is proud and ambitious, but her ambitions are not for herself but for her husband, whom she devotedly loves in spite of his faults of character.* BRANDON *rises. The three ladies curtsy, all surface politeness to one another.* ELLEN *withdraws.*)

SUFFOLK. Your Grace.
NORTHUMBERLAND. Your Grace—and Lady Brandon. This is a pleasure doubled. (*She rises from her curtsy and moves to* SUFFOLK. *They kiss.*) And such a sweet morning.

(NORTHUMBERLAND *makes no attempt to kiss* BRANDON. *She crosses, below* SUFFOLK, *to the window and looks off into the garden.* SUFFOLK *follows her to* R.C.)

SUFFOLK. It is indeed beautiful.
NORTHUMBERLAND. Your garden, my dear, is more lovely than ever. It is finer than ours.
SUFFOLK. Oh, no! You are too kind—though it is fair enough.
BRANDON. What a pleasant arrangement for you both—your new houses so near each other, separated only by the river.

(*She sits on the downstage end of the window-seat.* SUFFOLK *sits on the upstage end.* NORTHUMBERLAND *sits between them.*)

NORTHUMBERLAND (*laughing*). Moving house is a great labour, yet the result is most happy here. So peaceful—the green lawns and the green water. (*To* SUFFOLK.) We must arrange a water-party for the young people—or will your little Jane not be persuaded from her studies? How is the child?
SUFFOLK. She is well, I thank your Grace.
NORTHUMBERLAND. I hear marvellous reports of her scholarship. 'Tis said she corresponds with all the great scholars of Europe—and in Latin.
SUFFOLK. With some of them. Jane is well enough.
NORTHUMBERLAND. The Princess Elizabeth, too, I hear, is making good progress with her Latin.
SUFFOLK. Cousin Elizabeth has made a virtue of necessity. (*Confidentially.*) Perhaps we might whisper that she finds some thought of virtue—however late—somewhat expedient.

(SUFFOLK *and* NORTHUMBERLAND *laugh.*)

Will your Grace take wine?
NORTHUMBERLAND. I thank you, no. I find wine breeds acid in the stomach this warm weather.
SUFFOLK. Indeed? My stomach, praise God, is never queasy. (*With a change of tone.*) About Elizabeth—'twas a sad scandal.

BRANDON (*disapproving of this talk*). A scandal three years old. And the child was truly more sinned against than sinning. A man with the looks and charm of Sudeley——

NORTHUMBERLAND (*interrupting*). And his lack of scruples...

BRANDON. ——might well have persuaded her to greater folly.

SUFFOLK. How do you know, sister, *how* great was her folly? In my opinion, 'twas as great as might be. There were rumours...

BRANDON (*interrupting*). Rumours? There are always rumours. And Sudeley lost his head.

SUFFOLK. Which Elizabeth might well have done—in another sense than that she did. Remember who her mother was. (*Complacently, after a slight pause.*) Well, *our* children are more strictly guarded.

NORTHUMBERLAND (*sweetly*). Yet your little Jane, also, was in Sudeley's care.

(SUFFOLK *starts to her feet.*)

SUFFOLK (*coldly*). Jane is very different from Elizabeth.

NORTHUMBERLAND (*sweetly*). Indeed, yes! So very innocent, with so little of worldliness. You keep her, perhaps, even too close.

SUFFOLK. No more than is necessary.

NORTHUMBERLAND (*in a sympathetic tone covering slight cattiness*). Ah, yes! The knowledge of Sudeley's true character must have been a great blow to you—after you had twice trusted your daughter to his upbringing.

SUFFOLK (*sharply*). She was attended in his house—and a mere child.

NORTHUMBERLAND (*rising, putting a hand on* SUFFOLK'S *shoulder*). Of course! And there could never be a breath against her. Of that, I am sure, you may be very confident. (*She begins to move* L., *drawing* SUFFOLK *with her.*) Well, the old troubles are over now, we will hope, and England may look for peace and prosperity at last.

BRANDON (*angrily, under her breath*). Peace and prosperity!

NORTHUMBERLAND (*turning at* R.C.; *with a searching glance but a tone of mild enquiry*). My Lady?

BRANDON. Nothing.

NORTHUMBERLAND (*giving her another shrewd glance, then turning again to* SUFFOLK). I come, my dear Duchess, anxious for you upon another count. Is it true that you have had ghostly visitations here in Sheen?

SUFFOLK (*withdrawing a pace; after a brief pause*). Ghostly visitations? (*She laughs.*) Does your Grace believe in ghosts and such Papistical nonsense? I do not.

NORTHUMBERLAND. 'Twas an idle tale, then? Spread by servants, belike?

SUFFOLK. It must have been.

NORTHUMBERLAND. I am glad to hear that. 'Twould be a pity

if any—earlier inhabitants had resented your presence here. Of the old monastery, I mean.

SUFFOLK (*acidly*). I do not see why anyone should resent our presence here—any more than the nuns who once occupied *your* house. (*She moves up* C., *to the cupboard.*)

NORTHUMBERLAND (*sweetly*). Indeed, no!

(ELLEN *enters quickly* L. *and curtsies. She is in some excitement.*)

ELLEN (*to* SUFFOLK). Your Grace...

SUFFOLK. Well?

ELLEN. A groom has come from the Princess Mary...

SUFFOLK (*tense*). Princess Mary?

ELLEN. She is on her way to visit you, and will be here directly.

(SUFFOLK *moves down above the table. She is shrewd, calculating.* NORTHUMBERLAND *and* BRANDON *watch her.*)

SUFFOLK (*turning up to* ELLEN). Then she will dine here. Go to the kitchen, Ellen, and advise them. But first send Lady Jane here to me.

(ELLEN *curtsies and withdraws.*)

NORTHUMBERLAND (*suggestively*). Your Ladyship has a broad tolerance.

SUFFOLK (*annoyed, but controlling her annoyance*). You mean?

NORTHUMBERLAND (*with faint sarcasm*). So notable a reformer, yet with such welcome for a Papist.

SUFFOLK (*coldly*). I have, perhaps, more tolerance than some.

NORTHUMBERLAND. For Papists—or princesses?

SUFFOLK (*bluntly*). I refer, madam, to your husband. When he —er—" took the place of " the late Protector, he promised a tolerance we have not yet seen.

NORTHUMBERLAND (*coldly*). Which *you* should not desire. But I perceive that your Grace is able to trim her sails to all winds.

SUFFOLK (*stiffening, barely controlling her anger*). May I ask your Grace to explain?

NORTHUMBERLAND. Is explanation necessary? (*She eases down a pace.*) I merely congratulate you, madam, upon your diplomacy—and would venture to suggest it as a subject for your daughter's study.

SUFFOLK. My daughter? Jane?

NORTHUMBERLAND. Ay. She has a singleness of mind which ignores the—shall we say?—advantages of diplomacy.

(SUFFOLK *glares at her.*)

But I must take my leave.

SUFFOLK (*coldly*). Already?

NORTHUMBERLAND. I came but to convey my sympathy in your distressful visitations. A hand bearing a bloody axe is no comfortable symbol in troubled times—when so many are unwise.

SUFFOLK (*moving above and* L. *of* NORTHUMBERLAND). I beg your Grace to give no credit to such tales. But I thank you for the neighbourly thought.

NORTHUMBERLAND. 'Tis nothing, nothing! My Lord joins me in goodwill to you and your good lord and your children.

(BRANDON *rises.*)

SUFFOLK. You are most kind. (*She makes a slight curtsy.*) Commend us to your very good lord.

NORTHUMBERLAND (*moving* L.). I will. We shall expect you shortly at Sion House.

(*As* SUFFOLK *moves to accompany her.*)

No. Do not trouble. I will find my way. Farewell. (*She turns at the doorway* L.)

(SUFFOLK *moves up* C., *following* NORTHUMBERLAND.)

SUFFOLK (*easing to* C.). Farewell, dear my Lady—and our thanks.

(SUFFOLK, BRANDON *and* NORTHUMBERLAND *curtsy.* NORTHUMBERLAND *goes off* L. SUFFOLK *stands looking after her, furious.*)

Arrogant brach! (*Turning to* BRANDON.) Ellen was at fault in bringing that news when she was here. Yet I am glad of it. It will give her somewhat to chew over with her upstart husband. (*She moves down to the table.*)

BRANDON (*moving to* L.C.). So far I agree with you. But we must not forget their power.

SUFFOLK. There are other ways to power.

BRANDON. As I said—perilous ways.

SUFFOLK. Pah! I've a head for heights. (*She moves above and* L. *of* BRANDON.) Jane should be here. You heard what that woman said of her?

BRANDON. There was some pertness, was there not, when Jane last met Cousin Mary?

SUFFOLK. For which Jane was soundly whipped.

BRANDON. Poor child! She is delicate . . .

SUFFOLK. Whipped! And shall be again, unless she make amends.

BRANDON. You boast of moulding her to the Reformed Church, and thrash her for not accepting a Catholic? Upon my soul, Frances . . .

SUFFOLK (*interrupting*). Catholic or Protestant—one never knows whose friendship may be useful. Jane must learn that.

BRANDON. Learn . . . (*She breaks off, paces down* R., *then turns up to* SUFFOLK *again.*) Learn to use others for her own ends—or, rather, for yours. (*Troubled, she crosses to* L.C. *below the table and sits.*)

SUFFOLK (*tartly*). To hear you, sister, one would not imagine I had a thought for Jane's interests. Her father and I have given her opportunities equal to her birth. Why do you suppose we put her into my Lord of Sudeley's care? Because she must in all things be the equal of her royal cousins and . . .

BRANDON (*swinging round to face* SUFFOLK; *interrupting, harshly*). Enough, sister! (*She rises.*) Am I such a fool? You let Sudeley have care of her, for the second time, because he paid you and your husband two thousand pound for doing it.

SUFFOLK. Oh! (*She takes a few quick steps down towards* BRANDON, *furiously, then checks.*)

BRANDON. A most valuable pawn.

SUFFOLK (*beside herself*). Before God, I . . .

BRANDON (*interrupting, glancing* L.). Quiet! Here is Jane.

(JANE *enters quietly* L. *Her dress is in striking contrast with that she wore in the Prologue, and makes her look very young. The others watch her as she crosses up* C. *and curtsies formally.*)

JANE (*to* SUFFOLK). You sent for me, madam.

SUFFOLK. You've taken your time a-coming. And you were playing the virginals again this morning. That is forbidden.

JANE. I ask your pardon, madam. I will not offend again.

BRANDON (*kindly; touched by* JANE'S *pathetic dignity*). Come and kiss your aunt, child.

(JANE *moves dutifully below the table to her and gives her a cold little kiss on her cheek.* BRANDON *embraces her, but* JANE *is unresponsive.* BRANDON *laughs kindly, intent on easing the situation for* JANE.)

Why, here's a cold little paddock! I declare you sit indoors over your books until there is no blood in you.

    (SUFFOLK *moves to the chair above the table, and sits.*)

JANE (*primly*). I am well enough, I thank you, aunt.

BRANDON. You should be in the garden, on such a day. (*She sits.*)

    (JANE *moves away to* R.C., *and up stage.*)

SUFFOLK (*harshly*). I sent for you, Jane, because your cousin Mary is coming here.

JANE (*turning; aghast*). Cousin Mary? (*She moves rapidly down* R.C., *then swings round to face the others.*) Here?

SUFFOLK. Why not?

JANE. A Papist? To this house? What will Master Aylmer say?

SUFFOLK (*angrily*). I do not ask the opinion of my servants.

JANE (*protesting*). And Master Bullinger—all the scholars in whom my father has raised hopes for Reform? What will they think of us?

SUFFOLK. Quiet! It is time you knew, Jane, that there are other matters for consideration.

JANE. What matters, madam?

SUFFOLK. For one thing, courtesy to your cousin Mary. The last time you had to do with her, you made a fool of yourself and me. She is a princess, remember.

JANE. I wish her no ill. I would she might be converted to the true faith.

BRANDON (*amused*). And she, being charitable, doubtless wishes the same for you.

JANE (*horrified*). Conversion to Rome? (*Controlling herself.*) She has been falsely taught. I would I could teach her to see the truth.

BRANDON (*in humorous protest*). Child, child! She is more than twice your age, and (*with a shrewd glance at* SUFFOLK) may soon be Queen of England.

JANE. Were she twenty times my age, and Empress of the World, she would still be in error and sin. (*Simply.*) And I should still tell her so.

SUFFOLK. Jane! You will behave as a younger cousin to an elder. While she is here, there is to be no talk of religious differences.

JANE. And do you suppose, madam, that *she* will not speak of them?

SUFFOLK (*rising; angrily*). Malapert wench! Haven't your scriptures taught you to obey your parents? Am I to box your ears?

BRANDON (*starting to her feet*). No, Frances! (*She goes to* JANE *and again puts an arm about her.*) Come, poppet! You must be guided. It is not always good to speak so openly—even the truth.

JANE (*obstinately, stiff within* BRANDON'S *arm*). Truth is always good.

BRANDON. There are things you do not understand, and some matters in which a little tolerance may go a long way.

JANE. Ay, madam. Tolerance in religion may indeed go a long way—towards Hell.

SUFFOLK. Enough of this debating! You will learn to hold your tongue before your elders, who are wiser than you. I give you an order. You will say nothing to offend your cousin.

JANE (*easing past* BRANDON, *towards* SUFFOLK; *still grave*). May I keep my room, madam, and so avoid the occasion?

SUFFOLK. No, you may not! That would be to insult a guest.

JANE (*losing a little of her self-possession*). But how may I . . . ? (*She breaks off, then suddenly turns to* BRANDON; *impulsively, clinging to her in childish appeal.*) Can you not help me, aunt?

BRANDON (*unhappily*). What can I do, child? In this you must be guided by your mother. (*Desperately.*) Oh, I'd have you more a child, still. You are hardly beyond your dolls, and yet ... (*She breaks off.*)

JANE (*recovering her dignity, gently disengaging herself from* BRANDON). Do not trouble yourself, madam, I give you thanks.

(*She moves quietly away up* L. *to the window seat and stands with her back to the others, a lonely little figure.* BRANDON *looks at her with sympathy.*)

BRANDON (*moving quickly to* SUFFOLK, *speaking quietly*). Let her come home with me for a little.

SUFFOLK (*angrily*). And so establish her in her wilfulness? No, sister. I have heard overmuch of you this morning, and I have something yet to say to Jane.

BRANDON. Be gentle with her.

SUFFOLK. Do you dare? Are you her mother?

(BRANDON *stiffens. She turns away from* SUFFOLK, *moves to* JANE *and puts a hand on her shoulder.*)

BRANDON. God be with you, child.

JANE (*turning; gravely*). And with you, madam.

BRANDON (*moving to* SUFFOLK; *coldly*). I would you might see my words as well meant. (*She crosses up* L., *and turns.*) Give you good day, sister.

(SUFFOLK *does not reply.* JANE *curtsies.* BRANDON *goes off* L.)

SUFFOLK. Come here, Jane.

(JANE *moves quietly down* C. *and stands before* SUFFOLK.)

The time has come for you to know your father's purpose and mine. We are not rich, but we have spared no expense in your education.

JANE (*primly*). For that, madam, I cannot be too grateful. And indeed I am grateful. I have done my best with my books. Master Aylmer and Doctor Harding ...

SUFFOLK (*interrupting, impatiently*). Phut! I do not speak of the praise of your tutors, nor the reading of Latin prayers. Do you think you are the daughter of nonentities? You have had the upbringing of a princess—ay, better than your cousins, I doubt not. What has it gained you?

JANE (*puzzled, enquiringly*). Madam?

SUFFOLK. Have you any of the qualities of Mary and Elizabeth?

JANE. I should not wish to have their qualities.

SUFFOLK (*angrily*). And that you shall, or I'll learn you! You are not yet too old for swingeing, though you stand there like a frozen geck in your pretended niceness. Nor for a week on bread and water, neither. (*She moves quickly above* JANE *to the window, swinging round there to face her, pouring out a torrent of words.*) Oh, I do not speak of Mary's Popery, nor of Elizabeth's hoydenish ways. I speak of that in them which makes them fit to rule England, should that fortune come to them, which God forbid! Bastards both, their own father named them, yet they have the spirit of princesses. And so have I. But you? For all I may do, outside your books you are a mammet, a mumpish thing, with no more character than a lump of marchpane.

(JANE *has remained quite still. Her prim dignity and quietness is in strong contrast with* SUFFOLK'S *lack of control.*)

JANE. I have endeavoured, madam, to be dutiful in all I may.

SUFFOLK. But m' life—and you are *my* child! A Tudor! Have you no answers that do not come from books?

JANE (*easing above the* L. *end of the table*). I live happiest in my studies, which my father and you commanded me to take up.

SUFFOLK (*striding back to* JANE, *taking her by the shoulders*). Books, books, books! Learning was necessary to your state—though I ha' done without it well enough. But that is not all; 'tis no more than the clothes you wear. Can you not see for what we try to shape you? (*She pauses, exasperated.*) Oh, I must be round with you ... (*She breaks off, releases* JANE, *darts quickly to the door* R., *then to the door* L., *looking off at each to make sure that no-one is listening there. Then she returns to* JANE, *standing over her, speaking impressively.*) Have you not known that you are to be the Queen of England?

JANE (*starting in terror, whispering*). Queen of England! Oh, I have prayed God to keep me from that! But no! Even after the King there are ....

SUFFOLK (*interrupting, swinging round so that their faces are close together*). Mary and Elizabeth shall not stand in your way, when you are married to the King.

JANE (*shrinking and retreating a pace up stage*). Married to the King—ah, no! No! (*Her control gone at last, she breaks from* SUFFOLK *and runs to the window-seat, throwing herself upon it, sobbing.*)

(SUFFOLK *looks at her for a moment, then moves up to her and stands over her.*)

SUFFOLK (*deliberately*). That is our purpose, and for that you shall fit yourself. Anyone but a moon-calf would ha' seen it long enough ago. Sudeley should ha' tutored you, but he was an impulsive fool. Now mark your behaviour, girl. Learn to hide your feelings and put on a pleasant face to your cousins. You'll need their goodwill. And for the love of heaven stir yourself to learn some of the bearing of a queen. Stop that snivelling, now, or you'll never rule a kitchen, far less a kingdom! Even you could not ha' thought that all our preparation was but to teach you to say your prayers. (*She turns away and moves up* C., *then turns again to* JANE.) And remember this: Northumberland is powerful. We need to move with caution.

(*She turns again and goes off* L. JANE *remains lying on the seat. A moment later* ELLEN *enters cautiously* L., *glances back over her shoulder, then runs to* JANE, *sitting by her, taking her in her arms.* JANE *relaxes in* ELLEN'S *embrace, regarding her as a mother and more naturally affectionate towards her than to anyone else.*)

ELLEN. There there, chuck! What is it? Your lady mother in her tantrums again?

JANE (*sobbing*). Oh, Ellen! I don't want . . . (*She breaks off, with sudden caution.*)

ELLEN. What, sweeting?

JANE. No matter.

ELLEN. There's nothing you may not say to me.

JANE (*looking up, forcing a smile through tears*). It's nothing, Ellen. I'm just weak—silly . . .

ELLEN. Pray God you keep something of that weakness. Too much ice and too few tears in you. Tears are good for us women, sometimes. Has she been hurting you again?

JANE. No, no, Ellen! We must not talk of that.

ELLEN. Must we not? I've seen your poor arms black and blue with her nips, often enough. But there—you're almost grown, now. And then you shall have your own home, your own husband—kindness . . .

JANE (*starting up*). No, Ellen! Not to be married! (*She crosses quickly to* C.) I'll not be married . . . (*She checks herself, and stands, panting, above the* R. *end of the table.*)

ELLEN (*rising, and moving to* JANE; *comfortingly*). Oh, but he'll be such a fine lover! Such a man he'll be!

JANE. Not any man.

(*She turns, looking at* ELLEN, *who smiles easily at her, not understanding* JANE'S *horror.*)

ELLEN (*patting her shoulder*). You'll see, poppet.

JANE. No.

(*She stands desolately, drying her eyes.* ELIZABETH, *dressed for riding, enters boisterously* R. *In either hand she carries one of the boots thrown out by* SUFFOLK, *displaying them humorously. She is in high spirits.* JANE *and* ELLEN *are startled by her entrance.*)

Elizabeth!

(JANE *moves to* R.C. *She and* ELLEN *curtsy, but* ELIZABETH, *dropping the boots, moves in a rush to* JANE *and embraces her.*)

ELIZABETH. Jane! Why, tears? And on such a morning? I hobbled my horse among the apple-trees, and climbed over the south wall. But Jane . . . What have you done to her, Ellen?

ELLEN. Nothing, your Highness—save to tell her that she works too hard at her books and should play more. (*She moves to* L. *of the chair above the table.*)

ELIZABETH. Marry, yes! (*She looks at* JANE.) As white as a smock. Slip your tutors, cousin— (*laughing*) as I do on every chance. I've slipped them now. Lord, can you imagine Ashley's face?

ELLEN (*seriously*). Have you come unattended?

ELIZABETH (*releasing* JANE). Without even a page. (*She moves to* L. *of* JANE.) Holiday, holiday, I said to myself, and slipped out o' the window in the dawn, taking that way to avoid argument. (*She laughs again and runs to the cupboard, takes up* SUFFOLK'S *tankard, sees that it has been used, replaces it and takes up another which she fills with ale from the jug.*)

ELLEN (*crossing to her, up* C.). Some wine, rather, your Highness...

ELIZABETH. No. I've a thirst.

ELLEN. 'Twould be more fitting than strong ale.

ELIZABETH. Not it. Your health, Jane. (*She drinks heartily, then puts down the tankard, laughing at* ELLEN. *Mocking.*) A young girl to drink ale? Oh, fie! Yet 'tis a good English drink.

ELLEN (*making the best of that; as she crosses down* R. *briskly*). Will your Highness dine here?

ELIZABETH. An your mistress invites me—and no-one catches me earlier.

(*As* ELIZABETH *drinks again,* ELLEN *picks up the boots, moves up, and puts them down,* R. *of the cupboard.*)

ELLEN. You have heard, mayhap, of the Princess Mary's coming?

ELIZABETH (*simulating surprise*). Mary here? Today?

ELLEN. At any moment.

ELIZABETH (*moving down,* R. *of the table*). This is a pleasure I'd not looked for. (*Unseen by* ELLEN, *she winks at* JANE.)

ELLEN. I'll go tell her Grace.

(ELLEN *curtsies and goes off* L. ELIZABETH *goes back to* JANE, *swinging her round boisterously, then plumping her down on the window-seat beside herself.*)

ELIZABETH. Smile, Jane! I'll tell you a secret. I knew my sister purposed a visit here, and saw a chance to meet her. As you may have heard—even in this seclusion—I've been something out of favour. I wish to mend that, and so must get at Mary.

JANE. Then you told Ellen a lie?

ELIZABETH (*amused*). A lie? What is that? Something that takes purpose from its background, and is justified accordingly—as a matter of policy.

JANE. A lie is a lie.

ELIZABETH (*gaily*). And a castle is most often won by surprise. There is my justification. Mary won't blame me. She is all kindness. 'Tis those about her would have us ever sparring like any gamecocks.

JANE. Kind, you say? A Papist? I have heard . . . (*She breaks off, shocked.*)

ELIZABETH. Rome or Reform? Mere expediency.

(JANE *is more deeply shocked.*)

As to what you have heard, let your heart judge, not your ears. If I were no more than is spoken of me— (*laughing*) I'd have been short of a head, long enough ago.

JANE (*surprised*). You can laugh at that?

ELIZABETH (*with a change of tone*). I can cry, sometimes—when I am alone. (*Then, chuckling.*) But I set my wits to work, and my wits were better than theirs. Shall we go into the garden? Play bowls? I have it! We'll take a boat on the river.

JANE. Alone? (*She rises.*) I dare not!

ELIZABETH (*amused*). What? You still allow your lady mother to whip you? Then fetch a lute and some madrigals.

JANE. I thank you, no, cousin. (*As she moves to* C., *slowly.*) I have been forbidden music. (*She stands by the table.*)

ELIZABETH. Forbidden? (*She rises.*) Marry come up! I'd like to meet the guardian, governess, tutor, councillor, devil or what-you-will who'd forbid me what I'd set my heart on.

JANE (*facing down* L.). There are things of greater worth.

ELIZABETH. Of greater worth than music? (*Thoughtfully, as she moves towards* C.) Ay—love, perhaps, or fighting. I would I'd been made a man (*momentarily serious*) as my father and mother wished.

JANE. I spoke of virtue.

ELIZABETH. Why, you're as bad as Edward. And, to read his letters, one would think him a Scots parson. (*Laughing.*) They should match you with him, and . . .

JANE (*breaking in, in horror*). No! (*She moves to the stool below the table.*)

(ELIZABETH, *still laughing, stares at her.*)

ELIZABETH (*misunderstanding* JANE'S *alarm*). You're right, cousin. Something of more manhood, eh? Have no fear. Get you grown a little, you'll ha' looks enough to find you a proper man.

JANE (*turning; horrified*). Cousin—you speak wickedly.

ELIZABETH (*still laughing*). Wickedly? Why, here's a pretty peat—when I'd oblige you!

JANE (*horror turning to anger*). You don't know what you say.

ELIZABETH (*moving to* JANE, *below the table*). 'Fore God, Jane, you are too much wi' these tutors, and they nothing but old women. (*Leaning towards* JANE.) But you are young; four years—or a generation—younger than I. You'll learn.

(*She puts a teasing arm about* JANE, *but* JANE, *blazing with anger, throws off the arm and moves* R. ELIZABETH *looks at her in humorous surprise, and turns up, above the table.*)

Hoity-toity ! (*She eases to* R.C.)

(SUFFOLK *enters* L., *hurriedly.* ELIZABETH *swings round to face her.*)

SUFFOLK (*moving to* C.). Her Highness . . . (*She turns, facing* L., *and curtsies.*)

(ELIZABETH *and* JANE *also curtsy as* MARY *enters* L.)

MARY (*surprised*). Why, Elizabeth . . . ! (*She checks, up* L.C.)
ELIZABETH. Mary ! (*Running to* MARY.) This is a surprise !

(*She is about to embrace* MARY, *but* MARY *holds her off for a moment, looking into her eyes.*)

MARY. To me it is. But to you—are you ever surprised, Bess ?

(*She looks at* ELIZABETH *for a moment longer, wary of her, yet kindly and understanding. Then she laughs her gruff laugh and kisses* ELIZABETH. SUFFOLK, *and* JANE—*who has become very stiff—watch them.*)

Yet, I am glad to see you. It is too long since we met. I hope you are well—truant.
ELIZABETH. And you too, sister.
MARY. As well, I thank you, as may be. (*She crosses her, to* SUFFOLK.)

(*They kiss.*)

SUFFOLK. Our house is indeed honoured. I have sent for the Duke.

(SUFFOLK *and* ELIZABETH *kiss.* MARY *takes a step towards* JANE.)

MARY. And my little cousin . . . ?

(*She holds out her arms, but* JANE *remains stiff and still.*)

SUFFOLK (*sharply*). Jane !

(JANE, *who can bear no more, turns suddenly and darts off* R. MARY *stiffens in anger. All are tense, looking after* JANE.)

CURTAIN.

SCENE 2

SCENE.—*A London street.*

On the forestage. *Galloping hooves are heard off* L. *The* 1ST *and* 2ND WOMEN *hurry on* R., *and cross quickly to* L.C., *looking off. The former has a basket of provisions, the latter a dead duck or rabbit clutched by the neck or ears.*

1ST WOMAN. Duke o' Northumberland's men. Wonder what they've caught them two poor cullions for ?

2ND WOMAN. Somebody said summat about coinin'. What's that?

(*The sound of hooves dies away.*)

1ST WOMAN. What?
2ND WOMAN. Coinin'?
1ST WOMAN. Makin' o' counterfeit money.
2ND WOMAN. What's counterfeit?
1ST WOMAN (*impatiently*). See here, gossip—if thy headpiece were a real headpiece, well, 'twould be real.
2ND WOMAN (*trying her best to grasp this*). Ay?
1ST WOMAN. But, seein' as 'tisn't, 'tis counterfeit, see? 'Cause real's real an' counterfeit's counterfeit, see?

(*The* 2ND WOMAN *gapes. This is beyond her. The* 1ST WOMAN *puts down her basket, grabs the duck, and flaps it impatiently in the* 2ND WOMAN'S *face, to point her words. During this, the* 3RD WOMAN, *a vast female hobbling on two sticks, enters* R., *and moves slowly to them, panting and wheezing.*)

Counterfeit money is bad money, crack-poll, the makin' o' which is agen the law an' ordinance.

2ND WOMAN (*still struggling for light*). But—'ow can my 'ead be agen the law an' ordinance?

(*She snatches back her duck and strokes it possessively. The* 3RD WOMAN *has now reached the others.*)

3RD WOMAN (*wheezing*). If bad money looks like good money, as you'll allow . . .

(*The other two* WOMEN *turn to her.*)

1ST WOMAN. Ay, if 'tis good bad money.
3RD WOMAN. An' y'r honest merchant'll give goods for it, not knowin' no difference . . .
1ST WOMAN. Ay?
3RD WOMAN. Then where *is* the difference? What do it matter? Money's money, all said, an' little enough on't. Why not make some more?
1ST WOMAN. 'Cause 'tis agen the law an' ordinance.
3RD WOMAN. But why? Why d' they take them poor scabs t' be 'ung an' cut an' drawed, an' all for makin' on't?
1ST WOMAN (*after hesitation, at a loss*). Oh, thy tongue goes like a beggar's clack-dish!

(*The* 2ND WOMAN *titters. The* 3RD WOMAN *glares and makes a threatening movement towards her. The* 2ND WOMAN *moves hastily a pace up stage.*)

This coinin', 'tis a great misusage—(*confidentially*) but not only among the likes o' them. (*She gestures off* L.) I've 'eard as the great nobles does it, too—even the Duke o' Northumberland.

3RD WOMAN. The Duke o' Northumberland's a good man.

1ST WOMAN. Nay! The good Duke o' Somerset, the late Lord Protector, were better.

3RD WOMAN. What? Him they 'headed an' buried atween Queen Nan Bullen an' Queen Katherine 'Oward? (*Cackling.*) A rogue atween two wantons. Pah! (*She spits.*)

1ST WOMAN (*obstinately*). You may talk, but my Lord o' Northumberland's the worse master. My Lord o' Somerset were honest —that's to say, 'e were no more dishonest than 'e need a-been. An' 'e did try t' stand out agen the greedy tykes as enclosed the common lands for the increase o' sheep.

3RD WOMAN. Sheep? Sheep y'rself!

1ST WOMAN. You may scoff an' you may sneer, but I asks you this: be we better off than we was in the good Duke's time, or wuss off? Look at us now. Where's the army gone? An' what about ships? They says ther' ain't no ships bein' built now.

3RD WOMAN. What do us want ships for?

1ST WOMAN. I dunno. But they says 'tis a great lack an' a great scandal.

3RD WOMAN. The late Lord Protector—the devil take 'im— were no friend o' the poor, for all you may say. You'll not deny as 'e were responsible for the laws?

1ST WOMAN. Well, somebody got t' be responsible for laws.

3RD WOMAN. 'Owever much 'e may or may not 'ave done about turnin' the poor off their bits o' land wi' the enclosures, 'e knew all about markin' the vagabonds 'e'd made of 'em.

1ST WOMAN. Markin'?

3RD WOMAN (*bitterly, taking both sticks into one hand*). Look at this. (*With her free hand she tears open her dress, exposing the old angry scar of a great* V *branded on her chest.*)

(*The* 2ND WOMAN *has been edging nearer, and now, with the* 1ST WOMAN, *starts back in horror.*)

1ST WOMAN. God A'mighty!

3RD WOMAN. That's y'r good Duke o' Somerset!

(*She covers her chest and hobbles off* L.)

2ND WOMAN. Lackaday! 'Tis a pretty coil, an' the poor young King like to die any minute.

(*She takes up her basket and begins to move off* L., *followed by the* 1ST WOMAN.)

They says 'e's gone as bald as a' old man, an' 'is nails as come off, an' 'e spits blood by the cupful . . .

(*They go off* L. *There is a brief passage of music, which stops as the* CURTAIN *rises on the next scene.*)

Scene 3

SCENE.—*The room in the Duke of Suffolk's house. An afternoon in May*, 1553.

The flowers have been changed, the boots removed, and sunlight from the garden is now shining through the window into the room.

When the CURTAIN *rises,* NORTHUMBERLAND *is standing up* C., *holding a piece of embroidery.* SUFFOLK *is at the door* L., *speaking to someone off stage.*

SUFFOLK (*pleasantly*). Then we will leave you, my lords, to your game. (*She turns and moves to* NORTHUMBERLAND.) Come, my dear, be seated. (*She takes* NORTHUMBERLAND'S *arm, and they move down to the table. On the surface, they are very friendly indeed now.*) Shall I ring for some wine ?

NORTHUMBERLAND. No, I thank you.

SUFFOLK. Ah, I had forgot! Your stomach. (*She directs* NORTHUMBERLAND *to sit in the chair above the table, then seats herself on the stool below it.*) You are still troubled with the sourness ? So much breeding, I doubt me not. I think that God should send no lady more than a dozen children—though I envy you all your fine sons. (*Thoughtfully.*) Had I but one ! (*She notices that* NORTHUMBERLAND *is looking shrewdly at her, and hastily changes the subject.*) Has your Grace tried your wine boiled with ginger and cinnamon, with sugar and a long pepper ? 'Tis kinder on the stomach. I have the receipt. I will have Jane copy it for you.

NORTHUMBERLAND (*beginning to work on her embroidery*). Your Grace is very kind.

SUFFOLK. You are industrious.

NORTHUMBERLAND. I like occupation for my hands.

SUFFOLK. I cannot bend my mind to't.

NORTHUMBERLAND (*gently, but with meaning*). Ah ! You are troubled about Jane ?

SUFFOLK. Troubled ? (*She pauses.*) 'Tis true she is overmuch given to books—yet such a pearl of learning.

NORTHUMBERLAND. I meant not that. (*Looking straight at* SUFFOLK.) Will your Grace forgive plain speech ?

SUFFOLK (*tense, but speaking with a pretence of pleasantness*). I will forgive any speech from you, my friend—nay, welcome it.

NORTHUMBERLAND. The men are speaking on the same matter—your daughter Jane.

SUFFOLK. Jane ? Well ?

NORTHUMBERLAND. I have heard some talk, this twelvemonth past, that she should marry the King.

SUFFOLK (*defensively*). And who better ? Jane's birth—and the religion of both . . .

NORTHUMBERLAND (*quickly*). True, true ! Who better, indeed, than little Jane—were the King in health. But—you will keep this secret ?

(SUFFOLK *nods.*)

My Lord has it from Doctor Owen that the King cannot last the summer.

SUFFOLK. He may mend. He's at a difficult age. Get him past his teens ... (*She breaks off.*)

NORTHUMBERLAND (*shaking her head*). He's in a rapid consumption.

SUFFOLK. Then the marriage should be hastened.

NORTHUMBERLAND. No, no! Think, my dear, what would be Jane's position, married and widowed.

SUFFOLK. Queen Dowager, at all events.

NORTHUMBERLAND. What? With Mary as Queen? And little Jane, as you know, has offended her more than once. I'd not envy Jane in such a case.

(*There is a pause.* SUFFOLK *sits looking before her.*)

(*Cautiously.*) What would you say to a deed that would set aside the claims of both Mary and Elizabeth?

SUFFOLK (*starting to her feet*). Set aside King Henry's will?

NORTHUMBERLAND. King Henry was in no good case when he made that will. Had not he himself set both Mary and Elizabeth aside, as illegitimate?

SUFFOLK. True. (*She crosses thoughtfully towards* R.)

(NORTHUMBERLAND *rises and joins her down* R.C.)

NORTHUMBERLAND. The stock of Henry Tudor is diseased. Look at Edward and Mary—and who can say that Elizabeth is normal? Your branch, from his sister, is healthy—and you have the stronger claim to the succession.

SUFFOLK (*tensely*). I myself—*myself* ... (*She pauses, looking down stage, seeing herself as Queen of England.*)

(*Unobserved by her,* NORTHUMBERLAND *smiles cynically, but lets the reference pass.*)

NORTHUMBERLAND (*moving close above* SUFFOLK, *speaking seductively into her ear*). Our families have grown together in friendship. My husband, as you know, has the King's confidence. What if there should be another will?

SUFFOLK. Ah!

NORTHUMBERLAND. As to your daughter Jane—what more fitting match for her than our youngest son?

SUFFOLK (*turning to* NORTHUMBERLAND). Lord Guildford Dudley?

NORTHUMBERLAND. Guildford, though I say it, is all a maid might wish for in a husband.

SUFFOLK. Ay, he's young, tall, handsome ... (*She pauses, thinking.*)

NORTHUMBERLAND. A good boy, and kind. True, he has not Jane's learning, but that's no matter. And he's scarce like to have his father's abilities, but . . .

SUFFOLK (*interrupting, eagerly*). The better for that. He'll be the more easily guided, he and Jane. (*Turning down stage, again looking into the future.*) They'd have a son—to succeed me on the throne . . .

(NORTHUMBERLAND, *behind* SUFFOLK, *again smiles cynically*.)

NORTHUMBERLAND. You see, my dear, the advantages of this union.

(SUFFOLK *moves up and looks from the window, thoughtfully.* NORTHUMBERLAND *stands watching her*.)

SUFFOLK (*turning down to* NORTHUMBERLAND). The setting aside of my uncle's will—would it not be treason?

NORTHUMBERLAND. The action of the most powerful party can never be called that.

SUFFOLK. Somerset thought the same—and Sudeley. Yet they came to the scaffold.

NORTHUMBERLAND. Who sent Somerset to the scaffold, powerful though he thought himself? My husband. Have no fear. He is strong enough to carry this through. With the King's signature he can persuade the Council. Cranmer will certainly back him.

SUFFOLK. Who knows? Cranmer is deep.

NORTHUMBERLAND. Cranmer must needs fear Mary. Her coronation would be his death-warrant.

SUFFOLK. And the people . . . ?

NORTHUMBERLAND (*with a laugh*). The people will do, as ever, what the loudest voice tells them to do.

(*For a moment longer* SUFFOLK *stands, considering. Then she moves eagerly to* NORTHUMBERLAND.)

SUFFOLK (*purposefully*). Let us go and join the men.

NORTHUMBERLAND (*taking her arm, moving* L. *with her*). The marriage should be very soon. There is no time for delay.

(*They go off* L. *For a moment the room is empty, then* ELLEN *enters* L. *and crosses to* R. *She carries a light summer hat and a cup of milk*.)

ELLEN (*looking off* R.). Where is the child? Lord, they are less trouble ere they can walk. (*Calling*.) Lady Jane!

JANE (*off* R., *at a little distance*). Yes, Ellen? (*Nearer*.) What is it?

ELLEN. Your milk, child. And something to cover your head. You'll have a fresh crop of freckles, else. (*Turning, she moves up* R.C.)

(JANE *enters* R., *bareheaded, carrying a book*.)

JANE. No matter, I'm just coming in. It's difficult to read in the garden, Ellen. There's so much space above and about one; so many things to watch—bees, butterflies, birds ... (*She moves up to the window-seat, sits, and takes the cup from* ELLEN, *obediently drinking the milk.*)

ELLEN. Of which it were better that you took more notice than of those outlandish black marks on pages. Lord! Sometimes I wonder whether you only pretend they mean anything.

(JANE *laughs.*)

Your mother was here but a moment ago, with her Grace of Northumberland.

JANE. I know. (*She finishes the milk.*) That's why I went into the garden. (*She gives the cup to* ELLEN.)

ELLEN (*taking the cup to the cupboard*). And his Grace is playing chess with your father—or pretending to be. (*Moving down above the table.*) There's something going on.

JANE. They are very friendly of late.

ELLEN. Ay. And junketings are welcome. There's a company of players coming to Sion House. We are all to go over and see them tomorrow.

JANE (*shocked*). Players? Play-acting is wicked.

ELLEN. No, my dear. Their antics will do you good. They'll make you laugh.

JANE. That they shall not, for I shall not see them.

ELLEN. You should learn to laugh more. (*Moving to* R.C.) You, who say you can read all this cleverness— (*indicating the book*) if it is cleverness—so easily, you don't learn the simplest things.

JANE (*thoughtfully*). The simplest things? (*She sighs.*) Is life so simple? Sometimes I am tempted to wonder whether God means that I shall laugh and look for happiness. The world is beautiful.

ELLEN. Of course He means us to laugh, or He wouldn't have given us the power of it.

JANE. No. I know that such things are folly; that God put folly into the world for our resisting. We should not waste our lives in idleness and laughter.

ELLEN. Child, you're wrong! Oh, there's times when I could kick that Master Aylmer and those other black-beetles of tutors!

JANE. Ellen!

ELLEN. And so I could! All this book-learning—what does it do for you?

JANE. How can I show you that, you who cannot read? It is another world—a calm and peaceful world, Ellen, where men have noble thoughts, not petty ambitions; a world that I can live in with good content until I die. Oh, I pray I may never have to leave it!

ELLEN (*indignantly*). And I pray that you'll soon be married out of it, and have children to give you something worth giving your mind to. That's what I ...

(*She breaks off, for* JANE *has started up and is staring at her in horror.*)

JANE (*whispering*). Never!

ELLEN. Come, child—'tis a natural thing for a young maid...

JANE (*running to* ELLEN). Ellen! (*She clings to her.*) I don't want any change. I—I love my life as it is... (*She breaks off, fearfully.*)

ELLEN. Like a bird in a cage, and as fearful. But there's no need to fear. Most of us go through it well enough. Come, come, now! Men aren't all so bad.

(JANE *breaks away from* ELLEN *and sits again on the window-seat, composing herself.*)

JANE. Has there been fresh news of—the King?

ELLEN (*surprised*). The King? How you do change the... (*She breaks off, enlightened.*) Oh, I see! (*Gravely.*) There's no need for you to fear that poor boy. I doubt he'll live more than the month. You'll never call *him* husband.

JANE. Poor Edward! I've made a new prayer for him.

ELLEN. New prayers or old, 'twill make no difference.

(SUFFOLK *enters quickly* L. ELLEN *turns and bobs.* JANE *rises and curtsies.*)

SUFFOLK. Oh, here you are, Jane! (*She waves* ELLEN *away.*) I've something to say to you.

(ELLEN *moves up to the cupboard.* SUFFOLK *moves down to the chair above the table and sits.* JANE *moves to* R. *of the table and stands there quietly, fearfully, waiting.* ELLEN *takes up the cup and goes to the door* L. *At the door she turns to give an anxious backward glance towards* JANE, *then goes off.*)

I've news for you. Good news. Your father and I have arranged a great match for you.

(JANE *starts.*)

You are to marry Northumberland's son, Lord Guildford Dudley.

JANE (*retreating a pace; fearfully*). Marry? No—I will not!

SUFFOLK. How now? A splendid young man, and your playmate.

JANE. Mother! I have never liked him.

SUFFOLK. Nonsense!

JANE (*her fear crystallizing into a desperate obstinacy*). You told me I was to marry the King—as my duty—to uphold the Reformed Church. As that duty—for the Church—I might have— (*faltering*) might have... (*She breaks off. Desperately.*) But Guildford is vain and worldly, and I should not profit the...

SUFFOLK (*interrupting, slapping the table, viciously*). Stop that babbling! The King is as good as dead. As to duty, you have a duty to your parents.

JANE. I am not for marriage—not to any man.

SUFFOLK. What? You'd be a saint, belike, a celibate, a sour virgin? Or a Romish nun? You'd lead apes in Hell, would you?

JANE (*obstinately*). I will not marry! (*Uncertainly.*) Oh, I—I cannot . . . (*Her voice dies off in a whisper.*)

(SUFFOLK *starts to her feet and stands facing* JANE. *The situation forces her to make an effort to control her temper. Succeeding for the moment, she puts an arm about* JANE, *draws the girl to her despite her stiff unwillingness, and tries to reason with her.*)

SUFFOLK (*pretending gentleness*). Child, child, why will you be opposite on this matter? It is a great marriage for you, and there is nothing to fear. Guildford Dudley is a good boy, and will be kind to you. Handsome, too—most girls would jump at the chance of him.

(*There is a pause.* JANE *makes no reply.* SUFFOLK *tries again.*)

What is it? Do you remember him as your playmate, lording it over you girls? He was a green boy then. You'll find him changed, poppet, as a lover. In that, for all men may think, the woman has the mastery, as you shall learn, soon enough. He will be at your feet. Oh, we'll have such a wedding! We must see to your clothes—and all in haste, for we'd have you married while the King is still alive. If we wait longer, all our bright colours will be spoiled by mourning. You'll be such a beautiful little bride—oh yes, we must plan in haste. Now let us go find your father, and the Duke and Duchess of . . .

JANE (*interrupting, stonily*). No, Mother!

SUFFOLK (*angrily*). What? (*Again controlling herself.*) And your wedding to be the finest of the year? (*She pauses. Barely keeping her temper, she tries a different approach.*) There is another matter—one you cannot yet understand, but which you should know. These are unquiet days, and only the powerful are safe in them. It is necessary that our house should join with Northumberland. Your marriage will cement that alliance. You cannot refuse this help to us. (*She pauses.*) Come now, Jane!

(JANE *suddenly drops to her knees, clinging to* SUFFOLK'S *skirts, desperately.*)

JANE. Mother! Do not ask this. I cannot—will not . . . (*In a whisper.*) Oh, I dare not!

SUFFOLK (*losing her control*). Cannot, forsooth, and will not? I tell you, my wench, you shall marry Guildford Dudley whether you will or no. Now, be sensible, and let us get to business.

JANE. Oh, I am afraid . . .

SUFFOLK (*cutting in, brutally*). So? We must try other means, must we?

(*She savagely boxes* JANE'S *ears, twice.* JANE *sinks to the floor, sobbing.* SUFFOLK *grabs her and drags her to her feet, shaking her, speaking very quickly.*)

God's blood! This is a pretty return for all we've done for you. Money poured out like water and nothing spared—the most brilliant marriage in years arranged, and you mammering (*mimicking* JANE) " Oh, spare me, Mother! I am for no man—I'll not be married— I'm afraid!" Pah! Do you think to avoid the common custom of all women? Do you think to make gecks and gulls o' your father and me—ay, and the Northumberlands, too? You'll be curst and opposite, will you, and make a nayword of us all? But I'll learn you! I'll swinge you! Before God, you shall ha' no ease till you come to your senses.

(*She is holding* JANE *so that their faces are close together.*)

JANE (*whispering*). Mother . . . (*She stares at* SUFFOLK.) Are you my mother?

SUFFOLK. Am I your mother, hilding? Well you may ask, who might ha' been got from a kitchen wench. Is this the granddaughter o' the Queen of France, the great-niece o' King Henry? Out upon you! Now will you be persuaded?

JANE (*terrified but obstinate*). No—no!

(SUFFOLK, *mad with passion, takes both the girl's hands in one of her own, with the other striking* JANE *savagely. She has swung round so that her back is to the audience and hides* JANE *from them.* JANE *is sobbing.*)

SUFFOLK (*between blows*). Now will you—now? You'll set yourself against me, will you? Oh, you shall come to't! I'll lock you in the cellar with the rats, you thing, you mammet! I'll break you . . .

(*Under the blows,* JANE *has sunk to the floor again, where she remains in a huddled heap, sobbing.* SUFFOLK, *panting from her exertions, releases* JANE *and straightens herself.*)

Now will you still be opposite? Shall I bid your father bring a whip?

JANE (*desolately*). No, no . . . Oh-h-h-h, mercy of Christ! (*She masters her sobs.*) I'll—do your bidding. (*She weeps afresh.*)

SUFFOLK. Then get up.

(JANE *drags herself to her feet, weeping and dishevelled.*)

Stop whimpering! Go now. Wash yourself and mend your dress. Make yourself fit to be seen by a husband.

(JANE *makes a great effort and controls her sobs, then she goes slowly to the door* L. *and off.* SUFFOLK *stands quite still, watching her.*)

CURTAIN.

This scene is not over-dramatized. It actually took place. The only difference was that Jane's father as well as her mother was present. Jane was beaten into submission, both of them giving her many " shrewd blows."

ACT II
Scene 1

SCENE.—*A London street.*
On the forestage. Wedding bells, off, at a little distance. The 2ND WOMAN *enters* L., *weeping ecstatically, carrying a rose. The* 1ST WOMAN *follows her, counting coins in her hand.*

2ND WOMAN (*enjoying her tears*). Oh, it were a lovely weddin' ! Oh, I do love a lovely weddin' ! Oh, next to a good funeral, there's nothin' like a weddin'. (*She checks at* C., *and turns to the* 1ST WOMAN.)

1ST WOMAN. Picked 'em up, I did. Silver sixpences. One—two—three—what comes after three ? But no use askin' you.

2ND WOMAN. I never got nothin', 'cept this rose. I were too busy enjoyin' myself cryin'. Oh, my eyes'll be fair scalded after this !

1ST WOMAN. You should 'ave been on the watch when they scattered the purses. Trust the Duke o' Northumberland not to line the streets too thick with 'is money. You got t' get in an' grab. (*She nudges the* 2ND WOMAN, *chuckling.*) That's what they'll be a-doin' of presently, after the bride's garters.

2ND WOMAN. Oh, she were a lovely little bride !

(*The* 3RD WOMAN *hobbles on* R. *and moves to the others.*)

1ST WOMAN. Didn't think 'er anything much. Small an' quiet. I'd rather 'ave 'im. What an 'andsome young man !

3RD WOMAN (*wheezing*). What's all the to-do ?

2ND WOMAN. What ? 'Aven't you been to the weddin' ?

3RD WOMAN. Weddin' ? What weddin' ?

2ND WOMAN. Don't tell us you don't know ! Oh, a very big affair—Lord Guildford Dudley an' the Lady Jane Grey.

1ST WOMAN (*chuckling*). Should 'ave thought you'd 'ave gone to the weddin' o' the son o' y'r bosom friend, 'is Grace the Duke o' Northumberland.

3RD WOMAN. I went to one weddin' once. That were enough. My own. Give me a good execution, any day. What was it like ?

2ND WOMAN. Oh, lovely !

1ST WOMAN. Magnificent 'd be the word. (*Eagerly, to the* 3RD WOMAN.) 'Tis said they'd got a whole lot o' stuffs—velvet an' such-like—as belonged t' poor Lady Somerset, the widder o' the late Lord Protector. Ay, an' jewels. Oh yes, magnificent ! Magnificent—that's the word ! An' ther's t' be free beef an' ale for three days.

3rd WOMAN (*interested*). Where?

1st Woman. Suffolk 'Ouse, in the Strand—an' Durham 'Ouse. An' look what I got. (*She displays her money.*)

3rd Woman (*taking the coins to look at them*). Five sixpences, eh? Scrabbled for, I s'pose? You was quick. Is it good money?

1st Woman. So far as I be concerned, 'tis.

(*The* 3rd Woman *holds the coins, which, in her excitement, the* 1st Woman *momentarily forgets.*)

2nd Woman. The bride wore cloth of gold, wi' a silver tissue mantle an' a green velvet 'ead-dress, all blazin' wi' jewels.

3rd Woman. H'm! 'Ardly see 'er under that.

2nd Woman. She was led by two young pages, wi' bridelace an' rosemary tied t' their sleeves, an' sixteen maids in white went afore 'er.

1st Woman. Oh, but the bridegroom! Oh, there was a young man! Oh, magnificent! (*Giggling.*) I wish I were in 'er shoes.

2nd Woman. Flowers all over the street. (*She displays her rose.*)

1st Woman. An' the Dukes an' Duchesses o' Northumberland an' Suffolk—you never saw such finery! King 'Enry an' all 'is wives never beat it. Young King Edward weren't there, o' course —too ill, poor lad. But the Princess Mary was.

3rd Woman. What about the Princess Elizabeth?

1st Woman. No. She didn't go. Reckon she don't like the Duke o' Northumberland. But she'd 'ave liked 'is son. Oh yes, she'd 'ave liked 'im, wouldn't she just! Got a' eye for a man already, they says she 'as.

2nd Woman. Make a good queen, she will, when the King dies.

1st Woman. But the Princess Mary'll be Queen, surely? She's eldest.

2nd Woman. What? 'Er? Spanish, an' a Papist.

1st Woman. Only 'alf Spanish. As for Popery—well, some thinks one way an' some another. This weddin' was a bit Popish, they says, for all the Northumberlands talks s' much about Reform.

3rd Woman (*who has slyly pocketed the coins*). Once you starts on religion, you talks all day. Ther' ain't nothin' so full o' words as religion. I must be goin'. God ye good den, gossips. (*She hobbles past them to* L.)

1st Woman } (*together*). { Good den.
2nd Woman }   { Don't forget the beef.

(*They move* R. *together. The* 3rd Woman *exits* L.)

1st Woman (*as they go; earnestly*). You must understand, neighbour, as these 'ere great weddin's ain't exactly what our'n be. Us, you may say, *chooses* our men. We 'ouldn't be foisted off wi' somebody chose for us. But the daughters o' kings an' dukes an' whatnot 'as to 'ave what they be give.

2nd Woman. She were very pale—the bride, I means.

1ST WOMAN. An' so'd you be pale. Although, mark you, she'd done better'n most as could a-chose for theirselves. (*She stops suddenly* R.C.) The coney-catcher!
2ND WOMAN. What?
1ST WOMAN. My money!

(*She gathers up her skirts, turns, and rushes off* L. *The* 2ND WOMAN *gapes, and follows her off. The wedding bells fade out. Sad music fades in and continues until the* CURTAIN *rises again.*)

SCENE 2

SCENE.—*The room in the Duke of Suffolk's house. The evening of July 5th, 1553.*

The flowers are again changed or are removed. Twilight outside the window dimly lights the room to R. *On the table is a bowl of fruit. On the chest is a sheathed sword.*

When the CURTAIN *rises,* JANE *is lying on the window-seat, sobbing. A book lies on the floor near her. She remains there for a moment, then sits up, wiping her eyes and trying to control her tears, but very unhappy. She sits quite still for another moment, staring before her. Then she starts at the sound of humming off* L., *rises and steals off* R. KATE *enters* L., *humming "Greensleeves" and carrying two candelabra. She moves down and places these on the table. Then, seeing the book on the floor, she crosses to it, takes it up and puts it on the chest. As she does so, she knocks off the sword, which falls with a clatter to the floor. She picks up the sword with distaste, morbid curiosity forcing her to draw it out a little from the scabbard. She shivers.*)

KATE. Ugh! Nasty things! Men!

(*She hastily pushes the sword back into the scabbard and leans it against the wall near the chest. Then she goes off* L., *to return at once with a lighted taper. She moves down to the table, and is just beginning to light the candles when* RICHARD *tiptoes on* L. *and moves down behind her, catches her round the waist from behind, and kisses her. She has gained experience and now appreciates the kiss, leaning back against* RICHARD.)

Ah! Richard!
RICHARD. If we were married, sweetheart, *you* wouldn't run away from *me*.
KATE. Ah—no! (*With a wistful little laugh.*) Much good talking of *our* marrying. (*Disengaging herself.*) But have a care! They mustn't find us like this.
RICHARD (*kissing her again*). I could give Lady Jane a few lessons.
KATE. That's my Lord Dudley's place.
RICHARD. Oh, him! He doesn't know how. That's clear

enough—or she wouldn't have come running home to mother.

(KATE *lights the candles, blows out the taper, and eases to* R. *of the table.* RICHARD *goes off* L., *to return in a moment with a tray on which are goblets and a vessel of wine which he places on the table.*)

KATE. You know, they aren't really . . . (*She breaks off.*)
RICHARD. What? (*He moves towards her.*)
KATE (*confused*). Oh, never mind.
RICHARD (*taking her hands, teasing*). Aren't really what?
KATE. Not properly married.
RICHARD (*laughing*). I thought as much! Lord or no lord, what a fool the fellow must be! (*He drops* KATE'S *hands, moves idly up stage and takes up the sword, lovingly drawing and handling it, speaking casually over his shoulder, really more interested in the sword.*) How do you know that?
KATE (*easing to* R.C.). I heard Mistress Ellen talking to her—to Lady Jane. (*She turns.*) They say the Duke and Duchess of Northumberland are carrying on about it something dreadful—ay, and her own father and mother. The language they use! I suppose it's not a sin for the nobility to use such words?
RICHARD (*laughing*). What about the marriage?
KATE. It seems, as soon as the wedding feast was over, the Lady Jane made the Duchess of Northumberland promise to let her come home. And here she stays. (*As she moves back to the table.*) Fancy a little thing like that defying them all. (*She turns to face* RICHARD.)
RICHARD. But that was weeks ago. (*Moving down* R.C., *testing the blade.*) And her husband's done nothing.
KATE. Oh, he's wept and implored and . . .
RICHARD (*interrupting*). Wept? What a man! (*He is practising passes with the sword.*) D'you know what I'd do? I'd come here and thrash her soundly.
KATE. You wouldn't!
RICHARD. Hasn't she asked for it? Besides, women like men to beat them. (*He takes her by the arm and raises the sword like a stick, in playful threat.*)
KATE (*laughing*). Don't you try beating me.
RICHARD. Mind you don't deserve it, then. (*He gently hits her with the sword.*) When you're married to me, you'll do as I tell you.
KATE (*her face close to his, laughing*). Shall I?

(ELLEN *enters* L. *and stands listening.*)

RICHARD. Anyway, when I'd beaten her, I'd throw her over my shoulder and carry her home.
KATE (*mischievously*). To bed?
RICHARD. To bed. (*He laughs and salutes* KATE *with the sword.*)

ELLEN (*moving down* L.C.; *severely*). Do you want a beating, Master Richard?

(RICHARD *and* KATE *give a start*.)

RICHARD } (*together*). { What....?
KATE   { Oh, dear! (*She goes above the table*.)

ELLEN. You're not too old for it, mind. Let me hear no more o' your scandalous gossip. Lady Jane came home because she was ill, that's all. (*Crossing below the table to* RICHARD.) And stop playing about with the Duke's sword. You'll be hurting somebody. Put it up, I say.

(RICHARD, *recovered, dances round her, feinting with the sword*.)

D'you hear me, young bully-rook! (*She drives him upstage*.)

(RICHARD *laughs, sheathes the sword and replaces it against the wall. Then he runs off* L. ELLEN *turns to* KATE.)

As for you, my wench, I've warned you before.
KATE. You needn't. We're in love.
ELLEN. Oho! We're in love, are we? Don't you think that's the very reason why you need warning?
KATE (*impudently*). No. I know how to handle men. I'm not Lady Jane.
ELLEN (*grabbing* KATE, *raising her hand*). Did you hear what I told young Richard?
KATE (*losing her impudence, frightened*). No! Not to me, Ellen! Good Ellen, no! That's what they do to her.
ELLEN (*quickly*). To whom?
KATE. Lady Jane. Her mother nips her, too. It's a shame!
ELLEN (*seriously*). It's none o' your business, baggage. Learn to hold your tongue. (*Releasing* KATE.) Now run along, and give me no more cause to...

(KATE *is running off* L.)

Stay!

(KATE *checks and turns*.)

Have you seen Lady Jane anywhere?
KATE. No.
ELLEN. She must be in the garden.

(ELLEN *goes off* R. KATE *slips down to the table, takes some fruit, giggles, and runs off* L. *For a moment the room is empty, then* ELLEN *re-enters* R. *with her arm about* JANE.)

Out there without a cloak! And the evening's chilly, though 'tis July. Summers aren't what they used to be.
JANE (*bleakly*). It's all right, Ellen. I'm well enough.
ELLEN (*drawing* JANE *towards* C.). You are *not* well! I'm sure I don't know what we shall do with you, so much trouble as you are!

Her Grace o' Northumberland is here in a storm of rage—and with your mother, too. (*Pleading.*) You can't go on like this, child.

JANE (*obstinately*). They promised me I should come home after the ceremony. (*She checks at* R.C., *standing* R. *of* ELLEN.)

ELLEN. Yes, then, because you made yourself ill with crying. But they didn't promise you should stay here for the rest of your life. You're married, now, and with a duty to your husband.

JANE. I've no duty to him. I don't love him—I don't even like him. They made me marry him for their own purposes, but that's done, and ...

ELLEN. Child, child!

JANE. Well, they wanted an alliance between the two houses. They've got that.

ELLEN. They'll want more than that ... (*She breaks off and turns, as* SUFFOLK *is heard off* L.)

SUFFOLK (*off; angrily*). But I tell you I can do nothing with the girl—nothing.

JANE (*alarmed*). My mother!

(JANE *turns and runs off* R. ELLEN *follows her off, in anxious haste. An instant later,* SUFFOLK *and* NORTHUMBERLAND *enter* L., *in a furious rage with each other.*)

SUFFOLK (*entering*). It's Guildford's place to make her obey him. By m' soul, one would think I *wanted* the wench still moping about here!

NORTHUMBERLAND. You, her mother, should have better prepared her for marriage.

SUFFOLK (*sweeping over to* R., *towards the window-seat*). Perhaps you, as her mother-in-law, can succeed where you imagine I have failed. (*Turning.*) You have my leave to try. I cannot think what has come over her. She was obedient enough when I had sole handling of her.

NORTHUMBERLAND (*following her to* R.C.). What less have you now? I've scarce seen her since the wedding-day. Where is she?

SUFFOLK. Shut away somewhere with some book. I know not.

(NORTHUMBERLAND *swings round, paces impatiently to* C., *and back again.*)

NORTHUMBERLAND. If one could know what is happening at Greenwich Palace!

SUFFOLK. There, surely, all is well. The King is dying at last, and his will made— (*with satisfaction*) cancelling King Henry's will and excluding Mary and Elizabeth from the succession.

NORTHUMBERLAND (*moving down* R.). My husband has his enemies. (*She stares out into the garden.*)

SUFFOLK. So have we all. (*She moves above the table, and sits.*)

NORTHUMBERLAND (*still staring out*). Cranmer, Montague and Cecil were hard to persuade to accept the King's new will, though they had it from his own lips. (*She turns to look at* SUFFOLK.)

And the people are uneasy. (*Pacing up* R.C.) I would Jane had been married to Dudley a year ago, and had a son.

SUFFOLK. There is time for that.

NORTHUMBERLAND. It would ha' pleased the people, and made certain the success of our cause. As it is, Princess Mary will not lightly be set aside. My husband is too optimistic, as I tell him. (*She moves near* SUFFOLK *and bends towards her, speaking more confidentially.*) Mary must be imprisoned in the Tower, and Jane proclaimed, as soon as the King is dead.

SUFFOLK (*starting to her feet*). Jane proclaimed? (*Staring at* NORTHUMBERLAND.) But the will named *my* male heirs before Jane's. As neither of us has a son, *I* am next in the succession . . . (*She breaks off, suspicion growing in her.*)

(NORTHUMBERLAND *laughs*.)

NORTHUMBERLAND. Your Grace has not heard, then, of the later will?

SUFFOLK. Later? What is this?

NORTHUMBERLAND. The King's last will, sealed under the Great Seal, names, in the succession, your heirs male——

SUFFOLK. Well?

NORTHUMBERLAND. —and afterwards *the Lady Jane* and her heirs male. (*Amused.*) So, as you have no son, Jane succeeds to the throne.

SUFFOLK (*furiously*). And I am passed over? By God, this is a trick of Northumberland's! It's false—false!

NORTHUMBERLAND. It is not false. Should I tell you such a thing, not being true?

SUFFOLK. It is his trick, to keep the power in his hands alone, excluding my family.

NORTHUMBERLAND. It does not exclude Jane.

SUFFOLK. Jane! A puppet—a pawn in his hands, like that boy we've married her to! Queen Jane—oh, yes!—with Northumberland driving her. Oh, I will have satisfaction . . . (*She makes as if to attack* NORTHUMBERLAND, *controls herself with great difficulty, and swings away down to the table, where she pours herself a goblet of wine. Her hands shake so that the vessel rattles against the goblet. She gulps the wine and pours more, then is suddenly quite still as an idea comes to her. She drinks again, and draws a deep breath.*) You may jet yourselves and think all shall go your way, but you've to reckon with me, my Lady. My husband may be no more than a straw in your husband's hands, but I am of more account, I'll have you know. (*She drinks deeply again, and sits in the chair above the table.*)

(NORTHUMBERLAND *eases towards her, standing just above her.*)

NORTHUMBERLAND (*calmly*). Your Grace can do nothing. The people of England would never accept *you* for their Queen. With

Jane there is a possibility. She is young and sweet, and the people cheered her marriage with my son. The people are romantic. They like such marriages. The marriage, indeed, is our strong card, for there is always the fear that Mary, once Queen, might marry a foreigner—Prince Philip, belike. Elizabeth, too, is headstrong, and might well bring England under some foreign yoke by marriage. Jane is an English rose, safe married to an Englishman.

(SUFFOLK, *who has listened to this with an unpleasant smile, interrupts.*)

SUFFOLK (*sneering*). Safe married, indeed? And your son—what do you see for him? A crown, perhaps? (*She chuckles.*) It is unwise, your Grace, to count chickens ere they are hatched.

NORTHUMBERLAND (*dangerously*). What does that mean?

SUFFOLK. We shall see. (*She rises, moves down to the door* R., *and turns.*) Your pawn against mine—but mine will become a queen. It is not only our husbands who play chess.

NORTHUMBERLAND. What you are, you owe to my husband.

SUFFOLK (*mocking*). And not to my own royal birth? Oh no, my Lady Northumberland!

NORTHUMBERLAND (*incautious in her anger*). What has been raised up may as easily be cast down.

SUFFOLK (*laughing*). Even the Duke of Northumberland, I think, would be hard put to't to reverse the course of his own plotting. Jane will be Queen, and I am Jane's mother.

NORTHUMBERLAND. Her husband...

SUFFOLK (*interrupting*). Pah! You have seen what influence he has with her.

NORTHUMBERLAND. And heard you say that *you* have none.

SUFFOLK (*with a pace or two towards* R.C.). But what if my inclination should turn to march with hers? I assure your Grace that Jane has no desire to make your husband the grandfather of a king.

NORTHUMBERLAND (*crossing quickly to* SUFFOLK). I must see Jane—I *will* see her! (*Disturbed.*) Oh, these fights and brabbles and differences, at a time when all hangs in the balance! (*She takes* SUFFOLK *by the arms.*) Is there no sense in you? Our two families, united, may brave the storm that the King's death will bring at any moment—at any moment! But divided...

(*She breaks off as* BRANDON *enters* L., *quickly, agitated.* BRANDON *is dressed for outdoors.* SUFFOLK *and* NORTHUMBERLAND *turn to her, neither pleased to see her.*)

SUFFOLK (*sharply*). You come late, Eleanor, and something abrupt.

BRANDON (*moving to* C.). Time presses. Frances—I have not been able to get to you of late. I must have word with you now. I have journeyed...

NORTHUMBERLAND (*interrupting, angrily*). There are more urgent matters, my Lady Brandon, than sisterly visits and confidences.

BRANDON (*angrily*). Very well. It need be no confidence. You shall hear it. Your neck is as fit for the axe as anyone else's.

NORTHUMBERLAND (*moving near* BRANDON). Now what flea has bitten you?

BRANDON. I'd ha' none o' your son for my daughter, and you know why. Frances, here, has been more foolish.

SUFFOLK (*interrupting, moving near the others*). I've told you, Eleanor . . .

BRANDON (*interrupting*). Listen to me. There is yet time—a little time. The King lives yet. Oh, are you all mad? Will you think of nothing but your self-importance? Can you not see that the people of England will never uphold the setting aside of the Princesses Mary and Elizabeth?

SUFFOLK. Enough!

NORTHUMBERLAND. The people will listen . . .

BRANDON (*interrupting*). Oh, get this mad will reversed. Be content with the power you have. Look to the favour of the Lady Mary's Grace and make ready to proclaim her Queen. (*To* NORTHUMBERLAND.) Seek your husband now and move him to this.

(NORTHUMBERLAND *laughs*.)

(*Earnestly*.) I beg you. For his sake, your son's, Suffolk's, Jane's . . . (*She breaks off, fearfully*.)

NORTHUMBERLAND (*calmly*). A pretty exhibition, by m' faith!

BRANDON (*desperately*). Your faith? Have you faith in Northumberland that he is God? Do you think he can move the people of England with your faith and his ambition?

NORTHUMBERLAND. With his power. I have faith in our destiny.

BRANDON (*moving down above the table*). This will mean house against house, faction against faction, another civil war. (*Turning to face* NORTHUMBERLAND.) Ay, a war that will leave your husband's head as bloody as the heads of Sudeley and Somerset.

NORTHUMBERLAND (*still calm*). I am amazed, my Lady Brandon, that a Tudor should have so little of vision or courage.

BRANDON. Courage, your Grace, is not foolhardiness. (*To* SUFFOLK.) Sister . . .

NORTHUMBERLAND (*interrupting*). You would do better in persuading your sister to make her peace with me, and your niece to fulfil her marriage vows. (*Impatiently*.) Oh, we waste time!

(*She goes quickly to the door* R. *and exits. She is heard calling, off.*)

Jane! Jane! Come here at once!

BRANDON (*moving to* SUFFOLK, *appealing, her hands on* SUFFOLK'S *arm*). Frances! Will nothing move you?

SUFFOLK (*unpleasantly*). Of a truth, sister, you will not. (*She drags her arm away from* BRANDON *and goes up to the window, looking off*.) What is she doing there, that serpent? Ah, there is Jane!

(*She laughs.*) My Lady Northumberland as suppliant. Come here, sister, and see.

(BRANDON *goes to the window.*)

Look. She follows Jane like a young starling following its mother with beak agape. (*She laughs again.*) To see the wench making a show of spirit!

BRANDON. Jane has more spirit than you think. You did ill to force her into this marriage.

SUFFOLK. I am the better judge o' that.

(JANE, *angry and obstinate, with her head up, enters* R. *and crosses quickly to* L., *not looking at anyone else.* NORTHUMBERLAND *follows her, protesting.* ELLEN *follows* NORTHUMBERLAND.)

NORTHUMBERLAND (*entering*). But I tell you, child . . . (*She breaks off at* R.C.)

BRANDON (*moving up* C.). Why, Jane—have you no greeting for your aunt?

(JANE *checks at the door* L., *turns and curtsies to* BRANDON. SUFFOLK *moves up* R.C. NORTHUMBERLAND *is below and* R. *of her.* ELLEN *is down* R.)

JANE (*stiffly*). I crave your pardon, madam. I had not seen you. I hope your Ladyship is well.

BRANDON. Thank you, my dear. And I hope that you have recovered your health.

JANE. I beg that your Ladyship will excuse me. (*She turns to go off* L.)

NORTHUMBERLAND. You must stay, Jane. This matter must be . . .

JANE (*interrupting, quietly but definitely*). Madam, I have done all that I felt to be my duty—to you and my parents.

NORTHUMBERLAND. You have done little of your duty to us. As for my son . . .

JANE (*interrupting*). I have no duty to your son. I married him on the understanding that I might leave him after the ceremony—your own promise, madam.

NORTHUMBERLAND. For a day or two, until you had recovered from the fatigue of the ceremony.

JANE (*moving down towards the* L. *end of the table*). That I should continue to live under my father's roof. Those were your words. And now it pleases you to forget your promise, and my mother forgets it.

SUFFOLK. Be content, Jane. You shall stay with me.

(JANE *starts.*)

I think you were better here.

JANE (*amazed*). Mother! (*She takes two or three quick steps towards* SUFFOLK, *then checks again, doubtfully. She cannot believe* that her mother's change of mind is due to any consideration of, much less affection for, herself.)

SUFFOLK (*after a triumphant glance at* NORTHUMBERLAND). I have given some further thought to the matter. You are too young to leave home.

NORTHUMBERLAND. Your thought comes too late. Jane's place is with her husband. The law and her promise both compel obedience. Her religion also. And she shall be compelled, doubt me not. These are no times for the cosseting of squeamishness.

JANE (*relieved, but still puzzled*). To stay here with my books . . .

(*She is interrupted by a sharp knocking on the door* L.)

SUFFOLK. Who's there?

(RICHARD *hurries on* L., *carrying a letter*.)

RICHARD (*bowing*). For my Lady Northumberland. A rider has come in haste from Greenwich.

NORTHUMBERLAND (*eagerly, with a pace towards* RICHARD). Ah!

(RICHARD *crosses down to her and hands her the letter. She takes it and rips it open. The others watch her tensely as she reads it.*)

(*To* JANE.) This concerns you. The King is failing fast. Northumberland writes that you are to be ready on a moment's notice to be taken to the Tower——

JANE (*aghast*). The Tower?

NORTHUMBERLAND. ——there to await your proclamation as Queen of England.

JANE (*dazed*). Queen of England? No! That is not for me.

SUFFOLK (*sharply*). Jane! You have known of this . . .

JANE (*horrified*). I have heard the words, but I have put the thought away, never believing that it would come to this. (*Sharply.*) No, no! I will not. The Lady Mary is to be Queen. Not I— oh, God! Not I . . . (*She sways.*)

(BRANDON *darts to her and catches her as she falls in a faint.*)

CURTAIN.

SCENE 3

SCENE.—*Outside a London tavern.*

On the forestage. A tolling bell is heard, and a buzz of excited voices, off L. The 1ST WOMAN enters L., carrying two large leathern tankards of ale. The 2ND WOMAN follows her with two three-legged stools which she places on the floor. The voices off fade out.

1ST WOMAN. That's right. Hums a bit in there. 'Ere's thy ale, gossip.

2ND WOMAN. Ah! (*She takes one of the tankards.*)

(*They sit and drink with noisy appreciation during the following scene.*)

1ST WOMAN. Ay, that be a drop o' ripe an' meller. I says t' Sam Taplock, I says: "Sam," I says, "us can't afford it of'n," I says, "an' when us gets it us likes it good. Leave the small stuff," I says, "t' them as can drink frequent." An' that's what Sam done, God bless 'n! Lord, I be forgettin'! Us should be a-drinkin' the 'ealth o' the new Queen.

2ND WOMAN. Long live 'er Grace! 'Oo is she?

1ST WOMAN. 'Oo is she? Now you be askin' me summat. Nobody seems t' know. It seems like you pays y'r money an' you takes y'r choice.

2ND WOMAN (*alarmed*). Money? I ain't got no money. (*Eagerly, clutching the other's arm and nearly throwing her off her stool.*) Gossip! Will they throw money about the streets again?

1ST WOMAN. 'Ere! Don't throw *me* about the street—nor yet my ale. (*Seriously*). Money? More like t' be 'eads throwed about the streets afore this is done wi'.

2ND WOMAN (*impressed*). 'Eads? 'Oose 'eads?

1ST WOMAN (*impressively*). 'Oo knows? But blood'll flow like wine.

2ND WOMAN. That won't be much, then, if 'tis no more than all the wine as we've seen flowin'. (*She drinks.*)

1ST WOMAN. Pah! I was speakin' metamorphic. (*Leaning towards the other, confidentially.*) I favours the Princess Mary.

2ND WOMAN. Why?

1ST WOMAN. 'Ave I got t' give a reason why for everything? Well, if you must know, for no more rhyme nor reason but that she was treated cruel when a child, by that father of 'ers. An' I don't like the Duke o' Northumberland—an' ther's a lot more as don't, neither.

2ND WOMAN. Princess Elizabeth was treated cruel, too. That old father o' theirs, old King Hal, 'e must 'ave been a fair one, 'e must. Choppin' off 'is wives' 'eads! Why did 'e do it?

1ST WOMAN. Well, if you'm a king an' you've got tired o' y'r queen, I s'pose 'tis a bit of a temptation t' send for the 'eadsman an' say: "Take 'er off! I weren't prop'ly married to 'er an' 'er child's a you-knows-what."

2ND WOMAN. Ay! Well, seein' as they started equal s' far as *that* was concerned, give me the Princess Elizabeth—God bless 'er!

(*The* 3RD WOMAN *hobbles on* L., *wheezing, and overhears them.*)

3RD WOMAN. Treason! Lady Jane's t' be Queen!

1ST WOMAN. Princess Mary!

2ND WOMAN. Princess Elizabeth!

3RD WOMAN. Tongues 've been slit for less 'n that. An' ears cropped, too.

1ST WOMAN. Don't you talk t' me, old coney-catch! Tryin' t' do a poor 'ooman out of 'er honest dues.

3RD WOMAN. Don't you coney-catch me, gossip! I told you

fair an' straight at the time as 'twas but a' oversight, a' accident. I just slipped the coins into my pocket unthinkin' like, listenin' t' you. Didn't I 'and 'em back immediate?

1st Woman. Ay—when I threatened t' throttle the life out o' you.

3rd Woman (*changing the subject*). Well, Lady Jane's goin' t' be proclaimed Queen, 'cordin' t' the last will an' testament o' the late King Edward, God rest 'im.

(*The tolling bell stops.*)

1st Woman. 'Oo told you that? Your friend, the Duke o' Northumberland, I'll warrant. (*She spits.*) An' you knows what they says about 'im, don't you?

3rd Woman. They?

1st Woman. Everybody.

3rd Woman. Not me.

1st Woman. Then everybody 'cept thee. They says 'e poisoned the poor young King.

3rd Woman. Don't you let nobody 'ear you a-sayin' that.

1st Woman. I don't care 'oo 'ears me. When the Lady Mary's Grace is Queen, 'e'll get what 'e deserves—what 'e give the late Lord Protector. She 'ates 'im.

2nd Woman. I don't s'pose the Lady Elizabeth likes 'n much, neither.

1st Woman (*draining her tankard and rising*). Like'n? Ther's nobody in England as likes 'n, 'cept a few fools. England's tired o' these great blowed-out families, the Warwicks an' the like, pushin' theirselves up an' stalkin' in their pride in places what they wasn't never meant to 'ave. What good be they? Good for armourers an' farriers, ay, an' gallows-builders an' the cormorants what robs the dead on the battlefields. Good for the twisty lawyers an' such cockroaches what gets fat on factions. But no good to honest folk. England wants peace, not war.

3rd Woman. Then I'll tell you this: if Spanish Mary once gets crowned there'll be war all right—war wi' France.

1st Woman. That's different. France is a way away over the water. Our pigs an' poultry—ay, an' our maids—is safe from the soldiery if the war's in France.

3rd Woman. Then what about the Papists? She's one o' them, right enough.

1st Woman. I'm not so sure as thy bully-rook Northumberland ain't a Papist as well, for all 'is cant.

2nd Woman. But the Lady Elizabeth's a good Protestant.

1st Woman. She's another deep one.

2nd Woman. I don't care! (*She jumps up, shouting loudly.*) God save Queen Elizabeth!

1st Woman (*louder*). God save Queen Mary!

3RD WOMAN (*bellowing, louder than the others*). God save Queen Jane !

(*The three continue to shout. The voices off are heard again, louder. The* 1ST WOMAN *grabs her stool, waves it and rushes off* L. *The* 2ND WOMAN *does the same and follows her. The* 3RD WOMAN *shouts again.*)

God save Queen Jane !

(*She hobbles off after the others. The shouting off grows louder and more confused. A joyful peal of bells is heard, off. The voices fade out. The peal of bells grows louder.*)

SCENE 4

SCENE.—*The anteroom to* JANE GREY'S *bedchamber in the Tower of London. The afternoon of July 10th, 1553.*

Across the R. *corner up stage is a wide arched opening giving on to a corridor. Up stage* L. *is the entrance to* JANE'S *bedroom. Up* L.C. *a narrow window is set in the thickness of the wall. Down* L.C., *set obliquely, is a rostrum with two or three steps leading up to it, and on it a chair of state with a very high back of cloth, with the royal arms of England emblazoned on it, and a canopy—or, alternatively, an ordinary high-backed, carved armchair. Against the back wall,* R.C., *is a refectory table with a vase on it. To* R. *of this table a halberd leans against the wall. A cupboard or sideboard is against the* R. *wall. Down stage, towards* R., *is a stool, and down stage* L., *against the wall, a small chest or table with another vase.*

(*See the Ground Plan at the end of the Play.*)

The pealing bells are still heard. It is a beautiful day and sunlight is shining through the window. As the CURTAIN *rises,* KATE *is arranging summer flowers and leaves in the vase on the table down* L. *Having finished this vase, she moves up to the refectory table and begins to fill the other vase with flowers and branches from a heap lying on the table.* RICHARD *enters* R.

RICHARD (*moving towards her*). Brrrh ! I don't like this place. It's cold and clammy, even on a summer's day.

KATE. That's the thickness of the walls.

RICHARD. And the ghosts.

KATE. I thought you didn't believe in ghosts.

RICHARD. I do—here. There's too much history in this Tower of London—nearly all unpleasant. Too many people come here to have their heads taken off, neatly or clumsily according to the skill of the headsman. Have you ever seen an execution ?

KATE. No ! Of course not !

Sc. 4]   FROST ON THE ROSE   45

RICHARD. Why "of course not"? Women do, you know. They love sights they can get for nothing, so they all flock... (*He laughs and moves down stage, taking up the stool and setting it down c., then turns back to* KATE.) In confidence, sweetheart, I've never seen one myself. I imagine it goes something like this——

KATE. Don't! (*She moves down a little,* L.C.)

RICHARD (*ignoring her protest*). —the condemned man—that's me—advances to the edge of the scaffold, dressed in the best suit he can afford, and addresses the crowd. (*He addresses the audience in mock-heroic style.*) Friends—and others. Unaccustomed as I am to public speaking, I feel that I must make something of an effort on this occasion, as I am—er—unlikely to have another chance. For that reason, too, I shall make no apology for the length of my speech. I come before you, good people, on a *grave* errand.

(KATE *laughs.*)

(*He turns and bows to her.*) When I was young, they said I was a chip off the old block, but now—alas!—I am about to be chipped on the old block... (*He waits for* KATE *to laugh, but she is serious now.*) That's just as good a joke as the other.

KATE. Be quiet, Richard! It's horrible!

RICHARD (*to the audience*). Very well. I shall not give you the remaining hour and three-quarters of my speech, in which I admit everything, forgive everyone, and expect God to forgive me. After a few appropriate prayers—designed to last as long as possible—I give a little money to the executioner and kneel before the block. (*He kneels above the stool, feeling for the edge of it.*) I'm supposed to be blindfolded. There's a nasty depression on the block, into which I put my neck. (*He rests his chin on the edge of the stool, making a horribly pious face over it, then suddenly laughs and springs to his feet.*) But I'd rather be the headsman. (*He goes up* R., *takes up the halberd, makes a grimly humorous business of rolling up his sleeves, spitting on his hands, taking the halberd some way up the shaft, heaving it up like an axe and bringing it down on an imaginary neck.*) Oh, poor fellow—missed! (*He makes another stroke, reacting humorously.*) Oh, dear! Not halfway through yet? What bone and gristle!

KATE (*horrified*). Richard—please don't!

RICHARD (*the halberd raised*). Very well, we'll pardon him. (*To the imaginary victim.*) You may get up, sir—oh, be careful of that head, or you may lose it.

(KATE *laughs at him. He stops fooling, leans the halberd against the stool, and darts to her, putting his arms about her and kissing her.*)

KATE. You shouldn't...
RICHARD. What? Not kiss you?
KATE. Not make fun of executions. They're too terrible!

RICHARD (*his arm still about* KATE). I can tell you something worse.

KATE. No!

RICHARD. Down below there— (*he points at the floor*) right down in the dungeons—there's the rack, the screws, the red-hot irons ...

KATE (*clinging to him*). No, no, Richard! Please don't! I can't bear it!

RICHARD (*laughing*). Sweeting, you're not called upon to bear it.

KATE. I can't even bear hearing about it. And besides, there's not all unhappiness here. Lady Jane's come here to wait her coronation. They bring all the kings and queens of England here for that.

RICHARD. And some of them—queens, anyway—for those other matters I mentioned.

KATE. Did you see the procession?

RICHARD. No. I was trying to persuade a varlet to persuade a lower varlet to grease my lord's boots. (*He moves down and replaces the halberd and stool in their former positions, then sits astride the stool, facing up to* KATE, *who is* C.)

KATE. Oh, it was lovely! Lady Jane—er—Queen Jane, oh, you should have seen her! She wore a green velvet dress with a gold pattern on it, and great sleeves; then she had a white coif, and she was, oh, covered in jewels!* Lord Guildford Dudley was all in white and gold. Oh, isn't he a lovely young man!

RICHARD. Silly girls might think so—evidently his wife doesn't. I find him conceited.

KATE. S'sh! He'll be King now.

RICHARD. Will he? I wonder.

KATE (*ignoring this remark in her excitement*). They walked under a canopy. Lady Jane wore high pattens to make her look taller. They must have been very uncomfortable, I think, but I suppose queens have to learn to be uncomfortable. Her mother carried her train.

RICHARD (*sarcastically*). That must have been nice for her mother!

KATE. When they came to the gates of the Tower, her father and mother stood before her and bowed three times, then walked backwards before her. Just think of that!

(RICHARD *laughs*.)

Now what's the matter?

RICHARD (*laughing*). I'm thinking of it.

KATE. It's nothing to laugh at.

RICHARD (*becoming serious*). No, it's no laughing matter. They're getting too far ahead with their importance. Can you keep a secret, Kate?

KATE. That depends on the secret. What is it?

---

* This was what Jane actually wore on this occasion. Alter the description if necessary to fit the dress which she wears in this scene.

RICHARD (*rising and moving to* KATE). Swear not to tell anyone. It's serious—something I overheard.

KATE. You men make too much of your seriousness.

RICHARD (*annoyed, moving up* R.). All right, you shan't hear it.

KATE (*consumed by curiosity, calling him back*). Richard! That was only a joke.

RICHARD (*turning*). A joke—about a matter of life and death for many. Just like a woman.

KATE. Life and death? What is it, Richard? I swear I won't breathe a word.

(RICHARD *makes a boyish throat-cutting gesture with his finger, which* KATE *solemnly repeats.*)

RICHARD (*going near to* KATE; *confidentially*). My Lord of Northumberland wouldn't let the Council announce the King's death to the public till some time afterwards.

KATE. Why?

RICHARD. Because he sent a letter, supposed to be from the King, to the Princess Mary. It asked her to come at once to the King's bedside and give him the comfort of her presence.

KATE. But what was the use of that, if the King was dead?

RICHARD. The Duke wanted to catch the Princess Mary, and shut her up here.

KATE. To imprison her? Why?

RICHARD. Because they say she's the rightful heir to the throne, and the people like her best.

KATE (*indignantly*). They don't, and she isn't. Our Lady Jane's much nicer and prettier. And the people shouted "God save Queen Jane" this afternoon.

RICHARD. A few of them—in the Duke's pay. I'll wager most of them were quiet enough. Anyway, the Duke didn't catch the Princess Mary that way. Someone warned her, and she didn't come to London.

KATE. Where is she?

RICHARD. Somewhere in Suffolk, I think. And they say people are flocking to her standard.

KATE (*alarmed*). Will there be war?

RICHARD. I don't know. 'Twill be exciting if there is.

KATE. Monster! (*She moves quickly away from him and up to the table, turning there with her hands pressed against the table behind her.*)

RICHARD (*moving up towards her; surprised*). What now, sweetheart?

KATE (*angrily*). Don't sweetheart me! War exciting? How like a silly boy!

(ELLEN *enters* R.)

ELLEN. What are you doing here, Richard? Out you go—

quickly now.   The Queen is coming.   (*She goes down to the cupboard* R.)

(RICHARD *exits* R.   KATE *has turned to her flowers and is finishing their arrangement.   Having done so, she starts to go off* R., *but* ELLEN *moves up, stops her, and draws her down* C.)

Wait.   Mistress Tylney isn't in there, is she ?   (*She points to* L.)
KATE.   No.
ELLEN.   Then I may need you.
KATE (*relieved to find that she is not to be scolded*).   Wasn't it a lovely . . .
ELLEN (*interrupting*).   S'sh !

(*She gestures* R.   *They wait for a moment, looking towards the entrance.* JANE *enters* R.   *She is magnificently dressed and wears high pattens which add to her height.   She enters slowly, tired but glowing with excitement.   She has gained new dignity and at the same time greater warmth of manner.*   ELLEN *and* KATE *curtsy as she crosses to the chair of state.   She smiles at them and gestures them to rise, then, suddenly forgetting her dignity, sits like a child on the steps leading to the chair.*)

JANE.   Oh, I'm weary !
ELLEN.   Your Grace . . .
JANE (*holding out her arms*).   Ellen—dear Ellen.   You are still my mother.
ELLEN.   Dear child.   (*She goes to* JANE *and stands above her, putting her arms about her protectively.*)
JANE (*laughing*).   These ridiculous pattens !   (*She pushes out a foot from her dress.*)   Oh, they hurt my feet, over all those cobblestones.
ELLEN (*to* KATE).   Her Grace's slippers.

(KATE *goes off* L.   ELLEN *goes down on her knees and takes off* JANE's *pattens.*)

JANE.   I've left all the others below.   (*Amused.*)   They hardly noticed my going, I think.   I'm not a— (*with a little, rueful laugh*) a very *noticeable* queen, Ellen.
ELLEN.   You're a very sweet one, child.   And I'm sure you'll make a good one.
JANE (*sighing*).   I wish I might—but I'm so young, and I never expected it.   One needs to be a very good and great woman to be a queen.
ELLEN.   Give yourself time.   You haven't got the feel of it, yet.

(KATE *enters* L. *with a pair of slippers, which* ELLEN *takes from her and puts on* JANE's *feet.   The pattens, looking pathetic and ridiculous, are left lying on the floor below the chair.*)

KATE.   Is that all, madam ?

JANE. Yes, thank you, Kate. You may go.
KATE (*shyly*). I hope you—your Majesty will be very happy.
JANE. Thank you, child.

(KATE *curtsies to* JANE, *backs up stage a little, then turns and runs off* R.)

ELLEN. There's one loyal subject.
JANE. I hope there are many. (*Thoughtfully.*) I wonder.

(ELLEN *rises.*)

They say the people want me, but—oh, Ellen! Last night I lay awake for hours and was horribly frightened—and wished they hadn't thought of me for Queen. I didn't want to be Queen.

ELLEN. Of course, it's all new and strange.
JANE. You'll stay with me, won't you?
ELLEN. Until I die, or you send me away. Your Majesty knows that.
JANE (*clutching* ELLEN's *hand*). I shall never send you away—but—don't call me things like that—your Majesty—when we are alone together. Please don't—I— (*she breaks off, uncertain for a moment, then controls herself*) I'm still terribly frightened, but—today I've been telling myself that I must be strong. If God intends that I shall be Queen—and I suppose He does, I must do His will, no matter how much I may dislike it.
ELLEN. You mustn't dislike it.
JANE (*in sudden longing*). Oh, if I could go home to my books! (*She clings to* ELLEN *and buries her face in* ELLEN's *dress for a moment.*)
ELLEN (*comforting her*). There, there, poppet!
JANE (*again pulling herself together*). No! (*She rises and moves down* C.) There is no time for that. (*She turns and moves up to the table, burying her face in the flowers there for a moment, then turns to* ELLEN.) It was so lovely on the river this afternoon, as we came from Westminster Palace.
ELLEN. Yes. It was a very grand procession. The barges—all the banners and bright dresses . . .
JANE (*quickly*). I don't mean that. (*She hesitates. More slowly.*) I mean the water, dappled silver and green and blue, and the meadows and gardens under the sunshine. The sky was so very big and blue and far away, and there were great white clouds like the fleeces of sheep.
ELLEN. It's a glorious day, certainly. And a queen, like a bride, should have . . .
JANE (*sharply*). A bride? Don't, Ellen! *He* was there by me. He smiled to the people and acknowledged their cheers. I think, indeed, they cheered for him far more than they did for me.
ELLEN. I'm sure they didn't.
JANE. But I don't mind that. My husband didn't smile at *me*. He's still angry with me because I—I . . . Oh, because he keeps asking questions I won't answer.

ELLEN (*gravely*). You'll have to answer them now.

JANE (*sadly*). I suppose I shall. (*Passionately.*) Oh, Ellen! If I were back in our old home at Bradgate, before there were thoughts of ambitions and . . . (*She breaks off, controlling herself.*) No—I must think of this afternoon. This afternoon I tried to think of England, and of my people, and all I might do for them—and—and how I mustn't be shut up inside myself any more, but must be part of all outside. And all the time I was feeling that Heaven was so high and blue and far away. It made me feel so small—so far unlike a queen. I couldn't help thinking of the Lady Mary, who would make a far better queen, and who must be so very disappointed. (*She moves thoughtfully down to the stool and sits.*)

ELLEN (*firmly*). The Lady Mary is a Papist. (*She moves above and* L. *of the stool,* R.C.) We want no more such on the throne of England. That's why you are Queen.

JANE (*sadly*). It's going to be very hard, Ellen. You see, I—well, except about my husband—I've never made any decisions for myself. And now I must.

ELLEN. You have the Council—the Duke . . .

(*She breaks off, uncertainly, for* JANE *has risen and drawn herself up. She has gained authority.*)

JANE (*crisply*). If I am Queen, I must be above the others. My word must be the last word, and it must be right. I must make up my mind what is right, and say it out plainly in front of them all. (*She moves* C.) Archbishop Cranmer will help me.

ELLEN. You must be guided by the Council.

JANE (*turning to face* ELLEN). Guided, yes. But they mustn't order me against my conscience. (*Regretfully.*) Oh, it's so very much easier to let oneself be ordered. (*She goes slowly up to the window and looks off for a moment, then puts her hands together and prays aloud.*) Oh God, if to succeed to this throne of England is indeed my duty and right, help me to govern this Thy realm to Thy glory. Amen. (*She bows her head over her hands for a moment, then turns down* C., *refreshed and glowing.*) Oh, Ellen! I wonder whether any other queen has ever had so much to learn? (*She goes to the chair of state, mounts the steps and sits on it.*)

ELLEN (*surprised by the change in her*). You're learning already. You've grown since this morning. Why, your Grace is beautiful—like a rose opening.

JANE (*smiling, shaking her head*). You mustn't make me vain.

SUFFOLK (*off* R.). Wait there, my Lord Treasurer. I will take it.

(ELLEN *moves down* R., *and turns, waiting. A moment later* SUFFOLK *enters* R., *carrying the crown on a cushion. She is followed by* NORTHUMBERLAND. SUFFOLK *is very pleased with herself.* NORTHUMBERLAND *is angry.* ELLEN *curtsies to them.* NORTHUMBERLAND *moves up* C., *barely controlling her anger.* ELLEN *goes off* L. SUFFOLK *moves* R.C., *importantly displaying the crown to* JANE.)

So here you are, Jane! We waited for you. The Lord High Treasurer has brought the crown for you to fit.

JANE (*firmly*). His Lordship might have waited my order.

SUFFOLK (*taken aback*). Order, child? Your order? But we shall arrange all for you.

JANE. I give you thanks, Mother, but I must now attend to such matters for myself.

NORTHUMBERLAND (*softly*). What? Already?

SUFFOLK (*sharply*). What is this foolishness? Remember that you are still the child you were yesterday.

JANE. No, madam, I am not. And I must try to learn that I am not—in all things, small as well as great.

SUFFOLK. By my soul, I . . . (*She breaks off, trying to control her anger.*) Well, as we have the crown here, let us see how it becomes you.

JANE. No, madam, I thank you. There will be time for that. I have no mind, now, towards trappings. I have many deeper matters to think on.

SUFFOLK. Trappings? And what matters, pray?

JANE. First, my own unworthiness. Second, how best I may serve God and England.

NORTHUMBERLAND. Heard you the like, ever? (*She watches* SUFFOLK's *discomfiture with pleasure, then speaks coldly to* JANE.) You need not hesitate to fit this crown. It will be yours.

JANE. As God wills, madam.

NORTHUMBERLAND (*moving a little down* C., *above and* R. *of the rostrum*). I mean that another will be made for the King.

JANE (*sharply*). For whom?

NORTHUMBERLAND. You know very well. I speak of my son.

JANE. Lord Guildford Dudley is not yet the King.

NORTHUMBERLAND. He is your husband.

JANE. That, alone, does not make him King.

NORTHUMBERLAND. What means this?

JANE. An Act of Parliament will be necessary.

NORTHUMBERLAND. An Act of Parliament? You—already—speak of Parliament as though 'twere in your pocket? Mercy o' God, what next? What next, I say? Are you, then, grown so large that you dispose of crowns?

JANE (*unmoved by* NORTHUMBERLAND's *tirade; seriously*). The crown, madam, is not a plaything for boys and girls. I cannot make Guildford the King. Nor would I, if I could, until the people choose him and Parliament approves their choice.

(SUFFOLK *is now enjoying* NORTHUMBERLAND's *discomfiture.*)

NORTHUMBERLAND. Heaven give me patience! *You* will speak so, forgetting who put you where you are?

JANE. I shall never forget that. If God put me here . . .

NORTHUMBERLAND (*interrupting*). I speak not of God, but of the Duke of Northumberland.

JANE. You mistake, madam. I would not be called to such a place by any duke or dozen of dukes. As to Guildford, he must wait. I have told him so.

NORTHUMBERLAND. There is that he will tell you, girl, and roundly—on many matters, and soon. To cap all, I hear that you would deny him a place at the high table for the banquet tonight.

JANE. Certainly, I will. He has no claim, yet, to such a place.

NORTHUMBERLAND (*raging*). By m' life! I've never heard of such a thing! (*She moves nearer to* JANE.) Can you not understand that, though you may have the appearance of Queen, it is my husband who holds the power? He holds you up. Without his hand you could not stay in your place an hour.

JANE (*calmly*). If that is so, madam, he must be the instrument of God. (*Suddenly passionate*.) Oh, I am weary of these arguments!

NORTHUMBERLAND. Arguments, arguments! (*She moves quickly above and* R. *of* JANE'S *chair*.) Who makes these arguments? Who but yourself? Put an end to them, by giving way to those who are best able to advise you.

JANE (*stubbornly*). What I have said, I hold to.

NORTHUMBERLAND. Then you shall e'en ha' the Duke to you, to teach you somewhat to your better management of affairs. Think you that a malapert girl is to be allowed yea and nay in matters of state? My husband and my son shall ha' the ruling of you ere you are much older, I'll vow to that.

SUFFOLK (*trying to control her delight*). Enough, your Grace! The child is weary and must rest.

NORTHUMBERLAND (*rounding on* SUFFOLK). Ay, you may pretend a concern for her you have not. This garboil is much to your liking, I doubt not. You and your man are now to cling to your daughter's shadow, are you? Or belike you are to ride to power on her back?

SUFFOLK. Your Grace forgets discretion. (*She gestures* R.) The Lord High Treasurer waits.

(NORTHUMBERLAND *starts angrily, goes to* SUFFOLK, *snatches the cushion and crown from her, and moves up* R. SUFFOLK, *furious, takes a quick step or two after her, then checks. After a moment's hesitation she turns and crosses above* JANE'S *chair*.)

NORTHUMBERLAND (*going off* R.). Take this, my Lord, and put it back in its place.

(*She goes off* R.)

SUFFOLK (*quietly, to* JANE). You have done well to defy her. God's wounds! You have inherited more of my spirit than I had reckoned on. (*She leans towards* JANE, *putting a hand on her arm.*

Confidentially.) Show a bold face to Northumberland, and where is his power? I and your father will uphold you.

JANE (*quietly*). What I do now, Mother, is for no concern of you, nor of my father, but because I know it to be right.

SUFFOLK (*eagerly*). That is what I tell you.

JANE. Your right, madam, and my right—what I mean by right —are very different. (*She rises passionately, standing on the steps.*) Oh, I will not have this grasping, plotting, intriguing! You look only to what you may gain for yourselves, yourselves, yourselves! (*She sweeps across down* R.C., *and swings round.*) If I am not here to sweep away such things, I had better not have come. (*She moves quickly over to the window and stands looking off, panting, struggling for control.*)

(NORTHUMBERLAND *enters without the crown. She is grave and controlled now. She moves up* C., *looking towards* JANE.)

NORTHUMBERLAND. There is a letter come from the Lady Mary. She has escaped to Kenninghall, and commands that her right and title to the throne shall be proclaimed.

(JANE *remains still, not turning.* SUFFOLK *moves up to* NORTHUMBERLAND.)

SUFFOLK (*uneasily*). What can she do?

NORTHUMBERLAND (*dryly*). Nothing—while my husband holds the reins. But do not deceive yourselves that you, or Suffolk, or all this chit's new-found impudence, can take his place.

SUFFOLK *and* NORTHUMBERLAND *stare at each other as—*

the CURTAIN *falls.*

SCENE 5

SCENE.—*At Framlingham Castle.*

On the forestage. A fanfare is heard, off, then cheering voices and shouts of " God save Queen Mary." MARY *enters, wearing a cloak. She may be attended by an* OFFICER, *bearing the royal standard in his left hand and a drawn sword in his right.* MARY *raises a hand for silence. The voices stop.*

MARY. My people. My royal father, King Henry of gracious memory, in his will named me as successor to my brother, King Edward. Now, my brother being dead—of what cause as yet we know not—there is a conspiracy of traitorous and seditious rebels, led by that wicked man, John Dudley, Duke of Northumberland.

(*Groans, off.*)

This man has suborned certain members of the Council, and has caused wrongfully to be proclaimed as Queen the Lady Jane Grey, whom he has married to his son, with intent to usurp power for himself and his family.

(*Groans, off.*)

Therefore, good people, escaping from his plot against my liberty, I am come to you in mine own person, entrusting my cause and my life to your allegiance. That I am the rightful and true inheritor of the English crown, I take all Christendom to witness.

(*Cheers, off.*)

That I do earnestly love and favour you, and all loyal Englishmen, I do assure you ; and your presence here at Framlingham this day assures me in return of your love and fealty.

(*Cheers, off.*)

To the King my father ye were always loving subjects ; therefore I doubt not ye will show yourselves so to me, his daughter, not suffering any rebel—especially this presumptuous Northumberland—to usurp the government of our person and our realm. Pluck up your hearts, good subjects. Like true men, stand fast with your lawful sovereign against these rebels, and fear not that, with God's help, we shall speedily bring them to overthrow.

(*Fanfare, drums, cheering and shouts of "God save Queen Mary," off.* MARY *and the* OFFICER *go off. The voices and the cheering fade out. The drums continue for a moment in the background as an ominous note of war. Then the clanging noises of pieces of armour and weapons are heard as they are taken into the Tower and thrown down upon the stone floor. These continue after the* CURTAIN *has risen on the next scene.*)

SCENE 6

SCENE.—*The anteroom in the Tower. The night of July 17th, 1553.*

When the CURTAIN *rises, the room is lit with candles.* JANE *is sitting listlessly on the chair of state. She is recovering from an illness, and is weary and suffering great discomfort.* KATE *is crouching on the steps of the chair, sobbing.*

JANE (*kindly*). Peace, Kate. All will be well. Richard will come back to you.

KATE (*looking up, tearfully*). But—oh, your Grace, they say there will be a great battle—and he *would* rush off with the Duke, into the thick of it. He's no more than a silly boy, though he thinks himself a man.

(JANE *is half occupied with her own thoughts.*)

I doubt he knows, even, how to handle a sword properly. And I don't suppose he thought to take a spare shirt with him, or a pair of hose—and him forever catching colds in's head. Men are so silly!

JANE (*gently, smiling*). But now you called him only a boy.

KATE. Boy or man, they're all as silly as sheep. (*Alarmed.*) Oh, your Grace, is there any danger? They say the Princess Mary has a great army already.

JANE. Rumours are always exaggerated.

(*The clanging noises stop.*)

KATE. But suppose . . . ? (*She breaks off, fearfully.*)

JANE (*quietly*). You must learn, Kate, to trust in God.

KATE. It's very hard. The Catholics trust in God, too. If there is only one God, is He the same for the Catholics as for us?

JANE. There is one God for all men. The Papists are in error in matters of doctrine. God, in His time, will teach them to see their error.

KATE. Then He must be on our side.

JANE. We cannot foresee His purposes nor try to question His ways. If, for His good reasons, the Princess Mary should win this battle, then we must bow to His will.

KATE (*rising, shaking her head*). No, madam, 'tis too much for me. Why, if there's only a matter of submission, I wish all men would bow to God's will. But then, if God expresses one will to the Duke of Northumberland and another to Princess Mary—and all at loggerheads . . .

JANE. No, no, Kate. Do not be deceived by appearances. I must have you taught to read, and then you can study.

KATE (*hastily*). I thank your Grace, but I doubt not I'm better as I am. If Richard were here again, and whole . . . (*She breaks off, on a sudden fear.*) Your Grace—suppose Princess Mary wins this battle?

JANE. I have told you . . .

KATE (*interrupting*). I mean—what will they do to us?

JANE. To you, nothing.

KATE. But—you?

JANE (*absently*). I have not considered it. There are more immediate matters.

(ELLEN *enters* R. *and moves down* R.C.)

ELLEN (*to* KATE). Why are you not about your work?

JANE. Don't scold her, Ellen. She is in love, and her sweetheart has gone to war. You may go, Kate.

(KATE *curtsies to* JANE *and goes off* L. ELLEN *approaches* JANE.)

ELLEN. Love! Sweethearts! Much you know about either, my Lady, when you won't . . .

JANE (*interrupting*). Ellen!

ELLEN (*shrugging*). Well, I've stopped that noise out there. The idea, I said, and your Grace so lately ill. Ordnance, if you please, great guns and small, armour, bows, bills and pikes, piles of gun-stones . . .

JANE (*sharply*). These things should have gone to the army, towards Cambridge.

ELLEN. Then, belike, the Duke's order has gone awry. I'm not surprised, and everything done in such a hurry, and all confusion within and without. Letters here, there and everywhere at home and abroad, and all these appointments to be made and papers to be signed. I'm sure I don't know what they want so many writings for. Hasn't anyone a head to remember a thing? If the Duke had been looking out for what the Princess Mary might be expected to do, instead of . . .

JANE (*wearily*). Leave it be, Ellen.

ELLEN (*concerned, taking* JANE'S *hand*). You are still weak. You should be in bed.

JANE. I am better now.

ELLEN. You are far from well, and mustn't overtax yourself. You don't realize how ill you've been, these past four days. And bothered all the time with all this business of state. Oh, this is a pestilent place, and I would we were out of it! The foul humours of these old moats and dungeons . . .

JANE (*interrupting*). 'Twas not the Tower.

ELLEN. Oh, I know you think you were poisoned, but . . .

JANE (*interrupting*). What else? And a strong poison, to take all the skin off my back.

ELLEN. Poor child! Has the salve eased it at all?

JANE. I am more comfortable now.

ELLEN. I'm glad of that. But poison? No. Even the Duchess of Northumberland would not dare. Besides, she'd be cooking her own goose if—if she succeeded. Where would she be—or that husband of hers—without you?

(*There is a pause.* JANE *looks straight at* ELLEN, *and then answers thoughtfully.*)

JANE. I'm not sure.

ELLEN. But they're nothing, alone.

JANE (*seriously*). Ellen—this is between us two. No-one else must know I asked it. (*She pauses.*) You've eyes and a shrewd head. Do you think the Duke of Northumberland is really a good Protestant? Do you think him sincere in his profession of faith?

ELLEN (*evasively*). How should I know, your Grace? These matters are beyond me.

JANE (*insisting*). Tell me.

ELLEN. Then—I think the Duke of Northumberland might well profess any religion to serve his own purpose.

JANE (*quietly*). Ah! (*She pauses.*) I think so, too. And if a pawn refuses to be moved as a pawn, and makes a queen's move . . . (*She breaks off.*)

ELLEN. Your Grace goes too deep.

JANE. If I'll not do what the Northumberlands wish, might they not seek another pawn? Certainly the Duchess hates me, if only because she finds herself mistaken in me.

(ELLEN *moves away from* JANE *and up* R.C., *bracing herself to speak further. Then she turns down to* JANE *again.*)

ELLEN. Hate or no hate—there's one thing you must give way on.

(JANE *stiffens angrily.*)

It's common sense and for your own happiness—yes, believe me it is —as well as for the good and peace of England . . .

JANE (*sharply*). Not that again—now.

ELLEN (*persisting*). But, child, you must see that you can't go on being married and not married. The sooner you have hopes of a son, the better your people will receive you. It is your plain duty . . . (*She breaks off.*)

(JANE *has started to her feet, stiff with anger. She descends the steps, moves up* C., *and goes off* L. ELLEN *looks after her.*)

I can't help it. That's the truth. (*She goes up to the door* L., *and speaks off.*) Will your Grace go to bed now?

JANE (*off*). Not yet.

ELLEN. Shall I heat your milk?

JANE (*off*). No, Ellen.

(ELLEN *shrugs.* SUFFOLK *enters* R. *She is alarmed and restless.*)

SUFFOLK. Ellen.

(ELLEN *turns and curtsies.*)

(*Moving to* C.) Has my Lord been here?

ELLEN (*moving to* SUFFOLK). No, madam. I've not seen his Grace since dinner. The Queen is within.

SUFFOLK. The Queen will keep. (*She grasps* ELLEN'S *arm, disturbed.*) Have you heard any news?

ELLEN. Nothing this five hours, madam.

SUFFOLK (*releasing* ELLEN, *moving restlessly to* R.C. *and back again*). There are rumours. Servants hear them soonest and gossip of them.

ELLEN. As your Grace knows, I am no gossip.

SUFFOLK (*moving down* R.). He leaves me at a time when—oh, I suppose he has a chessboard out somewhere. And so much to be done. (*She turns back to* ELLEN, *urgently.*) They say the nobles and gentry of Norfolk and Buckingham have risen for Mary . . .

ELLEN (*interrupting, gesturing* L.). The child in there . . .

SUFFOLK. What of her? 'Tis her concern as well. (*Full of her own fears.*) They say more: there is unrest here in London. The people hate Northumberland—'fore God, I believe they hate him worse than the Pope. The townsfolk were silent and sullen. They gave him no cheer as he rode out. With hostility before and behind him . . .

ELLEN (*interrupting, quietly*). Consider your daughter's ears.
SUFFOLK. Pah! (*Continuing to air her fears.*) At Norwich they have proclaimed Mary, 'tis said. (*She catches* ELLEN'S *arm and draws her up* C.) Ay, and more—they say she has already an army of thirty thousand men.

(NORTHUMBERLAND *has entered* R. *and is standing in the entrance. In contrast with* SUFFOLK, *she is calm and confident.*)

NORTHUMBERLAND. Untrained rebels with hedge-bills and hay-prongs. (*She laughs grimly.*)

(SUFFOLK *and* ELLEN *swing round to face her.* ELLEN *bobs.*)

Your Grace enjoys the spreading of ill news. (*She crosses deliberately to the chair of state, mounts the steps and sits.*)

(SUFFOLK, *aware too late of her purpose, darts a few steps after her, then checks, angrily.*)

(*Firmly.*) But you may spare your fears.
SUFFOLK. I am not afraid.
NORTHUMBERLAND (*curtly*). You may spare your fears, I say. These yokels may drink ale and turn England upside-down with their voices—but, at the first sight of a cannon, they'll go running to hide in their own ditches. Northumberland will make no hardship of dispersing such a rabble led by a woman. Leave to him the conduct of that affair. We have our own to settle. (*To* ELLEN.) You may go, Ellen.
ELLEN (*annoyed*). I am in *the Queen's* service, madam.
NORTHUMBERLAND. Then go and serve her.
ELLEN. And this is her room.

(*She goes off* L., *angrily.*)

SUFFOLK (*to* NORTHUMBERLAND). And that her chair. Your Grace was never backward in setting herself up.
NORTHUMBERLAND (*calmly*). Then I suppose we must appear to be alike in that. (*Sarcastically.*) 'Tis pleasant to find some point of resemblance.
SUFFOLK. Is this a time for jesting?
NORTHUMBERLAND (*dryly*). I do not think the subject of our relations, my lady, will ever be a jest. (*She rises.*) But let be. (*She descends the steps of the chair.*) We must agree that mutual advantage lies in toleration. Our families, as you should need no further telling, must cling together. (*As she moves down* R.C.) Now that Jane is over her greensickness . . .
SUFFOLK (*interrupting*). She does not think it greensickness.
NORTHUMBERLAND (*turning; swiftly*). Whatever it was, *I* did not cause it, so enough of that. And she must now be persuaded out of these delays. By m' faith, my lady, I think it a poor thing that the succession to the throne should rest on the whim of a frozen girl.

[Sc. 6] FROST ON THE ROSE 59

SUFFOLK (*moving up to the window, and looking off, anxiously*). Cooped up in this great place we know nothing, see nothing. (*Turning.*) Have you no despatches from the Duke?

NORTHUMBERLAND. None, as yet. He has more to do than write letters. (*She moves up* C.) But we must have news *for* him, ere he returns. Jane must be brought to reason.

SUFFOLK (*easing down a pace*). Then get your own news! Your scheming, and your husband's, has put my daughter in my place. You may think to rule her and England through your son, but I tell you Jane thinks otherwise.

(*There is knocking, off* R.)

NORTHUMBERLAND (*turning to look* R.). Who's there?

(SUFFOLK *moves towards* NORTHUMBERLAND. *They stare tensely at the entrance* R. RICHARD *hurries on* R. *He wears a cloak and riding boots, and is wounded, exhausted and stained with mud. He crosses down* R.C., *and bows quickly.*)

Well?

RICHARD (*urgently*). Word—for the Queen.
NORTHUMBERLAND (*quickly*). What is it?
RICHARD. Where is her Majesty?
NORTHUMBERLAND. Come you from my Lord?
RICHARD. Ay—and no.
NORTHUMBERLAND (*suddenly moving nearer to* RICHARD, *anxiously*). Your news? Is there some mischance? Is my Lord—hurt?

(JANE *enters* L., *crosses swiftly to* C., *and stands on the steps of the chair of state. She is followed by* KATE *and* ELLEN. RICHARD *turns from* NORTHUMBERLAND *and runs to* JANE, *dropping on his knees before her.*)

RICHARD. Your Majesty—I ... (*He breaks off, distressed.*)
KATE. Ah! He is wounded!

(*She makes as if to go to* RICHARD. ELLEN *restrains her.* NORTHUMBERLAND *and* SUFFOLK *have moved a little down stage*, R.C. ELLEN *and* KATE *have moved in and are standing above and somewhat to* R. *of the chair.*)

RICHARD (*with difficulty*). Madam—all is lost.
JANE　　　　　　　　　　(*softly*). Lost?
SUFFOLK　　} (*together*). { (*fearfully*). Ah!
NORTHUMBERLAND　　　　　The Duke ...!
RICHARD (*rising painfully, and looking towards* JANE). The Duke of Northumberland has been taken.
NORTHUMBERLAND (*sharply*). Taken? (*She pauses. She controls herself with an effort.*) How comes that? Was there a battle?
RICHARD (*turning to* NORTHUMBERLAND). No real battle, madam. An ambush—a skirmish.

NORTHUMBERLAND. Then?

RICHARD. His Grace's men deserted to the Lady Mary.

NORTHUMBERLAND. Traitors!

RICHARD (*in greater distress*). Not they alone! The Duke retreated to Cambridge—and there—at the Market Cross—in a great crowd of people, he—he filled his cap with gold pieces and tossed it in the air, crying "God save Queen Mary."

SUFFOLK (*furious, terrified*). Ah!

NORTHUMBERLAND (*furiously*). 'Tis false! (*She darts to* RICHARD *and takes him by the throat, shaking him and forcing him to his knees.*) You come here with such a tale! My Lord would not—would not . . .

JANE (*sharply*). My Lady!

(*She puts a hand on* NORTHUMBERLAND'S *shoulder, pushing her away from* RICHARD. NORTHUMBERLAND *swings round and moves down* R.C., *where, deeply shocked, she stands with her back to the others. All are tense and silent.*)

(*Calmly.*) Continue, Richard.

RICHARD (*rising*). The people didn't believe him. They stood sullenly and didn't cheer or anything. They didn't even stoop to pick up the Duke's money. And there he was in the rain, with his red cloak bedraggled and his head bare. Oh, he was a proud man—and then to be brought so low.

NORTHUMBERLAND (*brokenly, to herself*). "God save Queen Mary," he said? (*Desperately.*) No! (*She turns towards* RICHARD. *Urgently.*) No! You were not there—you speak from hearsay. Tell me the Duke is taken—is dead—but not that. It was not my Lord, but another who said that. Think, now—not my Lord—Arundel, mayhap?

RICHARD. No, your Grace. The Earl of Arundel was before him and had already gained a pardon. It was Arundel who arrested him and broke his sword.

NORTHUMBERLAND (*brokenly*). Oh!

RICHARD. I was there and saw it all. That is the truth. (*He staggers up stage.*)

(KATE *darts to him and puts her arm about him, holding him up.* NORTHUMBERLAND *backs away from* RICHARD *and drops on to the stool, covering her face with her hands. Knowledge of her husband's treachery is worse to her than the news of his arrest.* SUFFOLK, *shaken by rage and fear, moves quickly to stand just above* NORTHUMBERLAND.)

SUFFOLK (*shrill as a fishwife in her fear*). Now we see the pattern of it! Those letters to the Emperor—the journey to Cambridge—the battle never fought—everything! This traitor had never intended to give battle to Mary. Oh no, he has deserted us and gone over to her. Deserted us! He could not have his way with Jane, so he'd discard her and set his hooks on Mary. Oh, the lying villain! He put all this in train, and then leaves us. And we, what are we to do now, with Mary marching on London? What? (*She turns* C. *and looks at* JANE.)

(JANE, *occupied with her own thoughts, takes no notice.*)

(*She swings up* C. *and down again to* NORTHUMBERLAND.) Oh yes, I can see it! And you uphold him! You and he cannot have Jane, so you turn to Mary. She'll be your hobby-horse, will she? Come what will, *your* nest shall be feathered.

NORTHUMBERLAND (*rising, sharply*). For the love of God, madam, shut your mouth and go. Return to your house, if you are afraid for your head.

SUFFOLK. And so I shall. Should I stay here like a rat in a trap? (*She turns to* JANE.) Come, girl.

(JANE *takes no notice.*)

No. Better not. Our ways are better apart—and you know who to blame for this.

JANE (*looking straight at* SUFFOLK, *quietly*). I know very well, madam, who to blame.

SUFFOLK. Not I—no-one has listened to me. (*Desperately.*) Oh, your father and you must look to yourselves . . .

(*She breaks off, turns and darts off* R., *deserting* JANE.)

JANE (*to* NORTHUMBERLAND). My Lady Northumberland . . .
NORTHUMBERLAND (*interrupting, speaking to herself*). John—I warned you, but you would not be warned. And now you—and our sons . . . (*She breaks off, again covering her face with her hands for a moment. Then she removes her hands from her face and turns to* JANE. *She has gained dignity in her grief. She moves to stand before* JANE'S *chair.*) I wished you no harm, child, though you withstood me. You do not know—you refused to know—what it is to love a husband; to love, though seeing faults and wishing otherwise. Ay, and not only my husband, but my five sons who are embrangled in this coil. I must go, to find out certainly what has happened.

JANE (*quietly*). Go, madam.

NORTHUMBERLAND. If this is true, I must to the Lady Mary, to beg her mercy for my husband and my sons. Ay, 'tis a wife's bitter privilege to put her pride in her pocket. As for you—I know not . . . (*She looks at* JANE *for a moment. Abruptly.*) Fare you well.

JANE (*still quietly*). Farewell.

(NORTHUMBERLAND *turns and goes off* R.)

ELLEN (*to* JANE). What now? Will your Majesty summon your Council?

JANE (*bleakly*). I have learned much, these last days. If I have learned anything of men, my Council will have gone the way of the rest—towards Mary. (*To* RICHARD, *sharply*.) Go to the Captain of the Archers of the Guard. Bid him lock the outer gates and bring the keys to me.

(RICHARD *bows and moves* R. KATE *runs after him, clutching his arm*.)

KATE. Don't leave me, Richard!
RICHARD (*impatiently*). What now? I shall return.
JANE. Go with him, Kate. Go, the pair of you, and lose yourselves in London.
KATE (*curtsying*). Oh, madam!

(*She bursts into tears and runs off* R.)

RICHARD (*to* JANE). I will return, your Grace, and . . .
JANE (*interrupting*). No, Richard. There will be no more fighting. You are best out of this. Kate needs you more than I.
RICHARD (*going to* JANE, *dropping on his knees*). If I can give my life . . . (*He takes* JANE'S *hand and kisses it*.)
JANE (*quietly*). I do not need your life.

(RICHARD *rises, bows, and goes off* R.)

Find my father, Ellen, if he is in the Tower.
ELLEN. Yes, my Lady.
JANE. If he is—I do not know. I've had small kindness of him, but perhaps at this time we should know each other better. (*She sighs*.) Well, bid him here if you can find him. And bid Archbishop Cranmer come to me. He will be faithful, and I need his comfort.
ELLEN (*going nearer to* JANE). Oh, child—if there were anything I could do . . .
JANE (*putting a hand on* ELLEN'S *shoulder*). I know, Ellen.
ELLEN (*taking* JANE'S *hand in hers*). Well, at least I shan't leave you. I'll do your errand and return.

(*Joyous peals of bells begin, off*.)

JANE. What are those bells?
ELLEN (*after an instant's hesitation*). I don't know. There are many steeples in London.

(*She curtsies and goes off* R. JANE *sits and remains quite still for a moment, listening to the bells, which are heard louder. Then she rises and moves up to the window, looking off, to* L. *The* 1ST WOMAN *enters* R. *She is wearing an apron and carrying an enormous fish. She moves timidly to* R.C. *and sees* JANE, *but does not recognize her*.)

1ST WOMAN (*bobbing*). Oh, mistress—is anybody about?
JANE (*turning*). I am alone here.
1ST WOMAN. Just my luck! (*Moving a pace towards* C.) Extra 'elp wanted in the kitchens, they said, to prepare for Queen Jane's coronation. So I applied for the job an' got it—tuppence extra not to be sneezed at and, between ourselves, good pickings. (*Suddenly*

alarmed, gesturing L.) The Queen's not in there, is she? Queen Jane, I mean?

JANE. No. (*She moves down, a little* L.C.) The Queen's not in there.

1ST WOMAN. I don't want 'er listenin'. Mark you, I can cook, when ther's anything to cook, which ain't of'n. But I never expected nothin' but a scullion's job, o' course—paunchin's an' pluckin's an' vegetables; then washin' dishes an' scourin' pots. They don't use the likes o' me t' cook for queens an' nobility. Oh, no! The Queen's cook is more important than the Queen.

JANE. Is he?

1ST WOMAN. Oh, ay! That fat cook Nicholas—d'ye know 'im, miss?

JANE. No.

1ST WOMAN. This very night—everybody bein' excited an' rushin' out t' see what all the goin's-on is about, an' nobody seemin' t' be ther' t' stop 'em—well, this Nicholas pushes this into my arms (*she indicates the fish*) for all the world like a newborn babby—an' tells me t' clean an' broil 'n for the Queen's supper. Then 'e goes off, too. (*She approaches near to* JANE. *The fish-head touches* JANE'S *sleeve.*)

(JANE *draws back a little.*)

Oh, I beg pardon, miss! Cold, ain't they? Smells, too. Well, t' get on wi' my tale—ther' was I left wi' this, an' all the rushin' an' confusion an' 'ullabaloo goin' past me. Then I finds myself alone in the kitchens, 'cept for deaf Jake, the boy, an' I says t' myself, "All gone from 'ere. Suppose they be all gone from upstairs, too, a-watchin' the sights? What be I t' do, then?" I asks myself. "An' time's a-gettin' on," I says.

(JANE *turns, moves up and looks from the window.*)

'Tis a problem, y'see, miss. If everybody's out, 'ow much o' this yer fish be I t' cook? Ther' ought t' be capons an' beef an' kickshawses as well, but . . .

JANE (*turning and interrupting*). Why are they ringing those bells?

1ST WOMAN. Oh, don't 'ee know that? They be for the Lady Mary's Grace—as is t' be Queen after all, they says.

JANE (*quietly*). For Queen Mary—already! (*She moves slowly to* L.C.)

1ST WOMAN. Oh, ay! London's pretty well solid for Queen Mary, now. Mind you, I don't know no difference atween 'em, 'cept as Queen Mary's a goodish bit older than Queen Jane. I saw Queen Jane walkin' in the procession, an' when she got married. I s'pose she'd be about the same age as you, miss—but a bit taller, I should think. But there, you'll know 'er well.

JANE (*sadly*). I wonder, of late, whether I know her as well as I should like to know her. (*She looks at the chair of state, as if seeing herself there.*)

1st Woman. Now that's nice, that is. That's charity, that is. 'Specially now.

Jane (*looking at the* Woman). Especially now?

1st Woman. They says ther's fifty thousand people outside the Tower.

(*The bells have stopped.*)

Jane. Fifty thousand?

1st Woman (*listening*). So quiet now, you wouldn't believe. Just standin' there, packin' together, waitin'. Just like folks do, waitin' for somebody to start. You stop a bit an' they won't be so quiet. They'll be shoutin' " God save Queen Mary," an', in the same breath, yellin' for Queen Jane's head.

(Jane *stiffens.*)

Mind you, I don't know what they wants t' do that for. Queen Jane's a nice little thing, an' 'armless enough, I'm sure. Only did what the Duke o' Northumberland told 'er. I wouldn't like 'er t' get t' know what I been sayin'. I wouldn't frighten 'er. (*Comfortably.*) But she'll 'ave t' know, soon enough, I s'pose.

Jane. She will have to know—what?

1st Woman. Well, if Queen Mary's the rightful Queen, an' that seems proved, Queen Jane, willy or nilly, must 'ave committed 'igh treason. Ay, the 'ighest sort o' treason—an' that's a 'headin' matter. Ay, she'll go to the block, sure enough, poor child. I wonder 'ow she's a-feeling' now? If I was 'er, I wouldn't be wantin' no supper.

Jane. If you were her, you would trust in the goodness of God.

1st Woman. Oh, ay! I've 'eard she's got religion pretty strong. (*Recalling her immediate problem.*) But what about this fish?

(Ellen *enters* R. *She starts as she sees the* 1st Woman, *then goes to her, grabbing her arm, dragging her away from* Jane.)

Ellen. What are you doing here, troubling her Majesty?

1st Woman (*aghast*). Majesty? But . . . Oh, I didn't know, I . . . As God sees me I didn't know. An' I said . . . Oh, what 'ave I said? Oh, dear, dear, dear . . .

(*She breaks from* Ellen, *bobs hastily, and scuttles off* R.)

Ellen. What has she said?

Jane. She thought me a maid-in-waiting. She told me that nearly everyone is out in the streets.

Ellen. It's shameful! And I can't find your father, nor the Archbishop.

Jane (*hurt*). What? Cranmer gone, too? (*She moves to her chair, and sits.*) A handful of guards, a few servants—perhaps. A few prisoners—and you and I, Ellen. That means, almost, you and

I alone—alone in this old place with all its history of blood. And outside is London, surging with people who shout as they are told —now for this queen, now for that—now Jane, now Mary. But the true Church, the pure faith of the Reformation—what is to become of that? Is England again to be shackled to Rome, and all we have gained be lost for a hundred years? (*She pauses for a moment. With sudden longing.*) Oh, Ellen! Do you think I might go home?

(*The bells begin again.*)

ELLEN (*sadly, shaking her head*). Not now, child. You... (*She hesitates.*) Well, you'd never get through the streets.

JANE (*quietly*). No, I suppose not. (*Wistfully.*) But, as it seems I can do no more here, it would have been pleasant to go home. Not to Sheen—to Bradgate. The forest there will be lovely now. (*She sighs.*) Perhaps the streets will be clear tomorrow?

ELLEN (*making a great effort to control her grief*). Yes, child— tomorrow—perhaps.

(ELLEN *stands looking at* JANE, *who sits quietly, looking very small and forlorn in the great chair of state. The bells are heard louder.*)

CURTAIN.

ACT III
SCENE 1

SCENE.—*The Anteroom in the Tower. The morning of January 25th, 1554.*

When the CURTAIN *rises, the sky outside the window is grey.* MARY *is sitting on the chair of state, reading from an inventory.* ELLEN *is standing* C., *listening to her.* ELIZABETH *is standing at the window, looking out. She wears a hat and cloak.* MARY'S *hat and cloak are lying on the table.*

MARY. Item: a large leathern box marked with arrows, once belonging to King Henry. In it, thirteen pairs of gloves, some worn, and two old shaving cloths.

ELLEN (*shaking her head*). No, your Majesty, we have not seen it.

MARY. A book of prayers, bound in purple velvet, garnished with gold. An English primer. Three old silver halfpence. Sixteen pence, two farthings, and two halfpence. A leathern purse with eighteen strange silver coins ...

ELIZABETH (*turning, laughing*). You keep strict account, sister. (*She moves down* R. *to the stool and sits, facing* MARY.)

MARY. We have had need. We have not been so well provided, you and I. (*She continues to read.*) A gold ring with a death's head. Three French crowns, one broken in two. A girdle of gold thread. A pair of silver twitchers. A pair of knives in a case of black silk ...

ELLEN (*interrupting*). On my honour, your grace, these things have not been here.

MARY. It is strange.

ELLEN (*indignantly*). You should know that my Lord of Winchester came before to demand them, and was insolent to my Lady Jane.

MARY. Insolent?

ELLEN. He accused my Lady of having sold some of the crown jewels.

MARY. Some were missing.

ELLEN. Then your Grace should have looked elsewhere for them. My Lady is honest, as you very well know. I have never seen her in such a rage as my Lord of Winchester put her in. She told my Lord to take all she had in personal possessions and begone.

ELIZABETH (*applauding*). Spirited, spirited! Where's the milk in Jane now? But 'twas unwise of her.

ELLEN. It was, indeed! My Lord robbed her of more than five hundred pound in gold angels and the like.

MARY (*gently*). Enough, Ellen! Lady Jane is a prisoner and her property is forfeit.

ELLEN (*her anger getting the better of her*). And this Winchester allowed to vent his spite on her, when he should be a prisoner, too! Ay, and so should many another who came crawling to your Grace to save their skins . . .

MARY (*sharply*). Ellen! You forget yourself!

ELLEN. I do not forget that poor child. Nay, I'll not be silent, if 'tis the last thing I say. The injustice of it! My Lord and Lady Suffolk go free, when they and the Duke of Northumberland were the prime movers in it all. And this poor young lamb, who never wanted anything but to stay at home with her books . . .

MARY. Peace, I say!

ELLEN (*ignoring* MARY). She is tried, condemned—ay, condemned to be 'headed or burnt at your pleasure——

(MARY *winces*.)

——and held here under that sentence. What did she do? Nothing but what she was forced to do.

ELIZABETH (*in friendly warning*). Have a care, Ellen. Your tongue runs too fast. You do the Lady Jane no good service.

(MARY *is gazing stonily before her, upset by* ELLEN'S *words*.)

ELLEN (*turning to* MARY; *suddenly changing her tone*). I beg your Grace's pardon, I—yes, my tongue runs away with me. But when I think of that child . . . (*She drops to her knees, appealing to* MARY.) Oh, your Majesty, you are kind. Everybody speaks of your kindness, even those who worked against you. Let my Lady go. She'd not harm you, even if she could. Let her out into God's air. 'Twill be spring soon, and—oh, if you knew how she yearns for the woods and primroses of Bradgate . . . (*She breaks off, wiping her eyes*.)

MARY (*kindly*). Your eloquence does you credit, Ellen, and your courage. But you are aware that your mistress has been fairly tried and found guilty of high treason . . .

ELLEN (*interrupting*). Ay, madam. But . . .

MARY (*stopping her with a gesture*). And for that there is but one punishment . . . (*She breaks off*.)

ELLEN (*passionately*). No, no, your Grace . . .

ELIZABETH. Quiet, Ellen! You may leave your mistress to the Queen's mercy.

MARY (*to* ELLEN). I have sent an order to Sir John Brydges that I will see the Lady Jane here. Go and attend her.

ELLEN. Your Grace will be merciful?

MARY (*cryptically*). Mercy must not be divorced from justice.

(ELLEN *curtsies and goes off* R.)

ELIZABETH (*rising*). Mary—you will never sign that child's death-warrant?

MARY. I pray God I never shall. But who can say what the folly of others may not do?

ELIZABETH. Folly?
MARY (*dryly*). You well know, sister, what that word means.
ELIZABETH. I? What mean you?
MARY. That you have not always been wise enough to keep your fingers from the fire.
ELIZABETH. Now before God I protest . . .
MARY (*interrupting*). Do not bring God's name into a perjury. I know well, Elizabeth, what part you have taken against me. And you should know that I am not a fool. One does not play hoodman-blind about the throne of England. You come riding to London to protest your loyalty, yet I am not sure that I should not have you, too, under lock and key.
ELIZABETH (*starting, between fear and anger*). Take my liberty—again?
MARY. Ay. Had our father found you in like case, you would have paid with more than your liberty.

(*There is a tense pause.*)

(*She sighs.*) Oh, there are still plots enough, and discontents. There are writings against the marriage I propose . . .
ELIZABETH (*interrupting, hotly*). The plots are all against your marriage, not against you. The people love you, but they will not have this Spanish Don Philip on the throne of England.
MARY (*angrily*). They shall have whom *I* will.
ELIZABETH. And they will not stomach the Inquisition here in London. Nor will they now acknowledge any Head of the Church other than the Sovereign of England.
MARY. His Holiness the Pope is God's Vicar on earth and the Head of the Church, here as elsewhere.
ELIZABETH. Your half-English blood, sister, has not given you a half-understanding of Englishmen. We are neither coerced nor compelled to any one faith or another. We worship as we choose.
MARY. Enough, sister! If there is heresy remaining, I shall burn it out.
ELIZABETH (*horrified*). Burn? Where is your kindness now?
MARY. Is it not kindness to burn the body that the soul may not burn?
ELIZABETH (*angrily*). Priests' talk!
MARY (*angrily*). Elizabeth! Have care o' your tongue.
ELIZABETH (*recovering, laughing*). Ah! Take my own advice given but now to Ellen. (*She moves to the steps of the chair and sits on them, looking up at* MARY.) Oh, a fig for quarrelling! You are Queen and must go your own way—and never believe that I would stand in that way, or do you any hurt. We are sisters and have this much in common—that we have both suffered grievously for the sake of our mothers.
MARY (*stubbornly*). Ay. But my mother was a great princess and virtuous . . . (*She hesitates.*)

(ELIZABETH *has grown tense and is about to explode again into anger. She controls herself, however.*)

ELIZABETH (*lightly*). Well then, mine was brave and beautiful. (*She leaps up and dances to the window.*) So what would you? (*She turns down to* MARY.) I protest, sister, I have no desire for your place. Give me a good horse and the clean air and English turf. (*She drops a curtsy.*) I am your Grace's most loyal subject.

MARY (*slowly, not looking at* ELIZABETH). I have been oft deceived. It is not easy for me to accept—oaths of allegiance.

ELIZABETH. Not even mine? The word of a princess and your sister?

MARY. Half-sister—and in that degree there is a whole sphere of difference. I tell you this, Elizabeth: I know of a certain plot of rebellion now ripening against me, and I bid you have care how far you may be embrangled in it. (*She is looking straight before her still.* ELIZABETH *is watching her tensely.*) You see that I love you well enough to warn you—for the sake of the two unhappy children we once were. (*She covers her face with her hands, wearily.*)

ELIZABETH (*in a low voice full of sincerity*). I have no hand— —nor ever have had—in any plot against you. I have no mind towards so high and lonely a place as that you have. Give me life and love.

MARY (*looking at* ELIZABETH, *wondering about her*). Lonely, you say—and love, you say? Then why do you deny me love and ease of my loneliness?

ELIZABETH. I do not.

MARY (*sharply*). You speak against the man I love.

ELIZABETH (*starting in surprise, moving down a few steps towards* MARY). The man you *love?* What? This Philip of Spain? But you have never seen him.

MARY (*taking a miniature from her breast*). I have his likeness— a noble likeness. (*She looks at the miniature lovingly, then replaces it.*)

ELIZABETH (*disgusted*). Noble—faugh! A man at once cold and lecherous.

MARY (*starting to her feet in a rage*). Elizabeth!

ELIZABETH (*lost to caution*). A man whose amours are the scandal of Europe, and who smears them over with a sickly piety—calculating —sneering. Able enough in politics, I doubt not, but—oh, in God's truth, *he* would gain much by this marriage. But you—ah!

(MARY, *unable to bear more, darts to* ELIZABETH *and stops her by striking her on the face.* ELIZABETH *cries out and starts back, her hand to her cheek.*)

MARY (*passionately*). You—with your slut's behaviour—*would* see things thus. Love! You do not read the word as I read it.

ELIZABETH. I am no slut.

MARY (*cutting in*). You learned your picture of love with the late Lord of Sudeley.

ELIZABETH. Lies, lies, lies!

(*Flaming with rage, she advances on* MARY, *who starts back to the steps of the chair. Then* ELIZABETH'S *Tudor caution and strength again come to her aid. She controls herself and stands stiffly with her hands at her sides, breathing quickly with the great effort she is making.*)

MARY (*shaken and ashamed*). Elizabeth! (*She drops on to the steps of the chair in a flood of tears.*)

(ELIZABETH *recovers and laughs.*)

ELIZABETH. Nay, sister! We're not a pair o' fishwives from Wapping. (*She goes to* MARY, *kneels, and puts her arms about her.*) Let us kiss and be friends again. Take the husband of your choosing, and God give you joy of him and a son for England. (*Her voice is warm, but her eyes are cold as she looks over the top of* MARY'S *bent head, and her expression is one of contempt and hatred.*)

MARY (*tearfully*). You are stronger than I. (*Wistfully.*) A son! God grant me a son.

(ELIZABETH *is smiling affectionately at her as she looks up. They kiss.* MARY *rises and sits again on the chair.*)

ELIZABETH (*lightly*). Words pass, and all's well again.

MARY. There is some mocking power in you, sister, a dancing devil, a will-o'-the-wisp I can neither catch nor counter. You've none of my inheritance of Spanish melancholy, and you can throw your dignity to the winds and your cap after it, yet never lose the first. I think you are more sprite than woman.

ELIZABETH (*laughing*). But now you called me slut.

MARY. I meant no more than anger. And you goaded me.

ELIZABETH. All's done. We'll not even trouble to beg each other's pardon. (*She moves down to the stool and sits.*)

MARY. There's a thing I must add to what I said but now. I have sent for the Duke of Suffolk to give him my commission.

ELIZABETH. Suffolk? For what?

MARY. To command my army against the rebels.

ELIZABETH. But—*Suffolk?*

MARY. Ay, Jane Grey's father. But I pardoned him.

ELIZABETH. As Ellen said, you might better have pardoned her.

MARY. This is his test of loyalty. Northumberland is dead and Suffolk free of his influence. He has a good chance to win Jane's freedom.

ELIZABETH. God grant he may succeed in that.

MARY. Amen.

(*For a moment they watch each other. For all* ELIZABETH'S *power of dissimulation,* MARY *does not trust her, though her kind heart makes her wish to do so. Then* MARY *sighs and takes a ring from her finger.*)

Elizabeth—this morning has shown that our father's temper lives in us both. Take this ring— (*she holds out the ring to* ELIZABETH) and, if you ever fall in my displeasure, send it to me to remind me of our love.

(ELIZABETH, *who is greedy and loves presents, has jumped up and darted to* MARY. *She takes the ring and examines it.*)

ELIZABETH (*delighted*). Mary! How beautiful! Oh, you were ever generous. (*She puts the ring on her finger, then kisses* MARY'S *cheek.*) Be assured that I shall never part with it.

MARY (*smiling, but grave*). I trust you never will—even to me.

(ELLEN *enters* R.)

ELLEN (*announcing*). The Lady Jane Grey.

(ELLEN *curtsies.* ELIZABETH *backs a pace or two above the dais.* JANE *enters* R., *curtsies, moves a few steps into the room and stands quite still, at* R.C., *waiting. She is calm and resigned.*)

MARY. Greeting, cousin Jane. I have come to see how you do.

(ELIZABETH *runs impulsively to* JANE *and takes her* L. *arm.*)

ELIZABETH. Good morning, Jane. Come. (*She leads* JANE *nearer to* MARY.)

JANE. God be with you, cousins.

ELIZABETH (*to* ELLEN, *indicating the stool down* R.). The stool, Ellen.

JANE (*quietly*). No, I thank you. It is customary for the prisoner to stand. (*To* ELLEN.) Wait in the corridor, Ellen, with the guards.

ELLEN (*curtsying*). I'll not be far away, my Lady. You may depend on that.

(*She turns, and exits* R.)

ELIZABETH. We have all been prisoners, Jane.

JANE (*quietly*). But not condemned.

MARY (*gently*). Enough, Elizabeth. (*To* JANE.) How are you, cousin?

JANE. I am well, I thank you.

MARY. And well treated?

JANE (*formally, making a report*). I am comfortable enough in the house of Mr Nathaniel Partridge, I thank your Grace, and am permitted exercise on Tower Hill.

MARY. Your household?

JANE. Lady Throckmorton, Mistress Tylney, Mistress Ellen and five servants, with an allowance of ninety-five shillings a week for myself and twenty shillings each for my attendants. It is generous.

MARY. Then you have no complaint?

JANE. I have one.

MARY (*kindly*). Ah—your lack of liberty? But you see that I must keep you here until all—storms blow over—at least ... (*Her voice trails off. She is the more uncertain of the two.*)

JANE. I do not complain of that—indeed, I should not, though I have no design against your Grace. I complain that I am not allowed a minister of the Reformed Church.

MARY (*schooling herself to gentleness*). That you cannot have, child. I have sent you good Doctor Feckenham in hopes that he may convert you to ...

(JANE *stiffens.*)

(*Hastily.*) You cannot complain of him. He is of all men the kindest and least bigoted.

JANE (*relaxing a little*). He is kind indeed, and we are friends— on all matters but those of religion.

ELIZABETH (*laughing*). On which, I have heard, the good Doctor provides you much food for argument.

JANE (*gently reproving*). This is no thing for laughter, cousin. And you, surely, are of my persuasion?

ELIZABETH (*after a brief pause, calculating, trying to laugh off an awkward situation*). I do not make so much of certain matters as do Mary and you. I'd not think that one of you was for Heaven and the other for Hell on some small point of doctrine.

MARY (*sharply*). Small matter? Transubstantiation ... (*She breaks off, controlling anger.*)

JANE (*to* MARY). Doctor Feckenham is hopeful still that I shall be persuaded to change my faith. But I tell you, madam, I will not—no, not to save my life.

MARY (*sadly*). You life does not hang upon this matter, Jane.

JANE. Will your Grace answer me a question?

(*There is a slight pause.* MARY *looks at* JANE *enquiringly.*)

What have you done with Thomas Cranmer?

MARY (*starting, angrily*). Cranmer? We will not speak of him.

JANE. He is a good man, and gentle. Let him not suffer ...

MARY (*furiously*). Bethink you, girl, of my mother, and of what this Cranmer did to her—the dishonour he put upon her and me. And spare your breath in his cause, for you might better use it in your own. Cranmer lives yet, that he may be brought to see the error of his ways and recant his heresies. But the rope and knife await him——

JANE (*hurt*). Ah!

MARY. —or the fire. Be sure of that.

(JANE *covers her face with her hands.* MARY *controls her anger and rises, moving down to* JANE, *putting her hands on her shoulders.*)

There! I'd not distress you. But you would not be stopped, child. Would you weep for Cranmer? He deserted you.

JANE (*taking away her hands, controlled again*). I do not weep. I was praying God to give him strength.

(*There is a pause.* MARY *looks at* JANE. *Each appreciates the strength of the other.* ELIZABETH *watches them.*)

ELIZABETH. You two—so alike, so different. If I'd the strength of either, I'd not be content with ruling half the world.

MARY (*thoughtfully, looking at* ELIZABETH). The world? In the *world*, perhaps, you may be strongest. But do not forget what I have said. (*To* JANE.) Your father will be waiting audience with me.

JANE (*surprised*). My father?

MARY. I have sent for him here upon a matter of some importance. It must not be delayed, so I must leave you for awhile—but I'd have you wait here with Elizabeth. I shall return soon.

(MARY *releases* JANE *and goes off* R. JANE *and* ELIZABETH *curtsy as she goes.* JANE *is thoughtful.*)

JANE. Why does the Queen send for my father?

ELIZABETH. He is to be given opportunity to prove his loyalty.

JANE (*bleakly*). Loyalty? I thought he had done that already. Did he not proclaim her Queen before I was ... (*She breaks off.*)

ELIZABETH. He took a sensible step to save his life. Northumberland tried to do the same—but he might have known it was useless for him.

JANE (*angrily*). Northumberland! Woe worth him! He brought me and my family to this pass, and then tried to save his own life by denying his faith and turning to Rome. That last I cannot forgive him.

ELIZABETH. Well, he is dead—with so many others. Though, if one thinks of it, Mary spared all she could. My father would have made a bloodier matter of it.

JANE. What of *my* father?

ELIZABETH. He is to lead the Queen's men against a new rebellion.

JANE. Another?

ELIZABETH. Men rise against this Spanish marriage.

JANE. And justly. Surely my father would not favour it?

ELIZABETH. Yet if, by obeying the Queen, he might save you ...

JANE (*interrupting*). How could he? With Prince Philip on the throne of England, I must certainly die.

ELIZABETH. There may be means. (*She goes to* JANE *and puts an arm about her.*) Take heart, child. Mary has no desire for your death. She resists the Council—ay, and the Emperor, though she wants him for father-in-law. And Philip of Spain seems in no haste to come to England. Mary is too old for his liking. (*She begins to pace to and fro down stage, leading* JANE.) All will be well, I am sure. But take the advice I have given you before—keep your religion to yourself.

JANE. That I shall not.

ELIZABETH. Learn diplomacy, child. You'd never have made a

queen. (*In a lighter tone.*) Do they let you see that husband of yours? No, I suppose not.

JANE. I have no wish to see him.

ELIZABETH. What? So very handsome! Such beautiful legs! I'll warrant he's a dancer. 'Tis time you grew up, Jane. 'Tis a pleasant young man, I have understood.

JANE (*directly*). When you marry, cousin, will it be for love or policy?

ELIZABETH. Policy, I doubt not. (*Laughing.*) But I'll see their choice is such as may bring love.

JANE (*puzzled*). " Such as *may bring* " . . . ?

ELIZABETH (*laughing*). Oh, Jane! We are not all of the stuff of saints or nuns. But enough of that. I would we had you out of here, and all well together.

JANE (*wistfully*). Ah! If I could but go home to Bradgate and . . . (*She breaks off.*)

(MARY *has entered abruptly* R. *and is standing in the entrance. She is furiously angry.* JANE *and* ELIZABETH *stand together* L.C., *looking at her.*)

MARY (*abruptly*). Suffolk is not here. He has joined the rebels. (*She crosses to the chair of state and sits, brooding.*)

(ELIZABETH *and* JANE *are tense, watching her. After a moment,* ELIZABETH *leaves* JANE *and goes up to the window, looking off.* JANE *moves quietly to stand before* MARY'S *chair, a prisoner again. She knows that her father's action has signed his death-warrant, her husband's and her own.* MARY *speaks to her, bleakly.*)

Have you anything to say?

JANE (*quietly*). Your Grace, there is nothing to say. I ask your leave to withdraw.

MARY. You may go.

(JANE *curtsies and goes to the door* R.)

I would have saved you.

(JANE *turns at the door. She curtsies again in acknowledgment, turns and goes off. There is a pause.* ELIZABETH *turns down to* MARY.)

ELIZABETH (*heavily*). I'd not be Queen, to sign away a woman's life—a child's . . . (*She breaks off, and looks sombrely at* MARY.)

MARY (*heavily*). You may yet be Queen—and with that to do.

(*She rises in sudden agony, going to* ELIZABETH, *taking her in her arms.*)

For Christ's love, Elizabeth, watch your own feet! These rebels would have you in my place before your time. But they must fail —and you . . . No! Not you as well as Jane . . .

(*She breaks away from* ELIZABETH *and goes off* R., *groping her way as if in tears.* ELIZABETH *stands watching her.*)

ELIZABETH (*thoughtfully, to herself*). Queen? (*She pauses, and then turns down stage.*) Ay—perhaps . . . But there must be no heart, or it will break. No heart—only head, and strong hands.

CURTAIN.

SCENE 2

SCENE.—*Outside the Tower. Just after dawn on February 12th, 1554. On the forestage. A dim light. The sound of hammering is heard, off* R. *The* 1ST, 2ND *and* 3RD WOMEN *enter* L. *The* 1ST, *who carries a basket, is excited; the* 2ND *is yawning; the* 3RD *still hobbles, wheezing, on her two sticks.*

2ND WOMAN (*yawning*). Aaah-ugh! So early to drag out o' bed.

1ST WOMAN. If you wants a good view o' the block, you've got t' be early. Any free entertainment'll attract a crowd—specially executions.

(*They move* R.)

Listen to them, busy on the scaffold.

2ND WOMAN (*shivering*). Lor', what a mornin'! I wish they'd do these jobs in summer.

1ST WOMAN. No pleasin' some folk. (*She cranes to look off* R.) Yes, we can see well from 'ere, if the guards don't stand in the way. The block will be about there, where they got that lantern.

3RD WOMAN. Will they do her first, or him?

1ST WOMAN. Oh, she won't come 'ere. They'll do her inside the walls. She's of royal blood, y' see. But Lord Guildford Dudley's a commoner. This is for 'im.

2ND WOMAN (*disappointed*). But I wanted to see her.

3RD WOMAN. So did I.

1ST WOMAN. So you shall, if you're quick enough. He's first. But you'd rather see 'em both, wouldn't you? We'll 'ave to stir ourselves an' push a bit, but 'twill be worth that. Oh, 'tis a sad thing, that lovely young man—an' little Lady Jane never even married proper to 'im, they says, poor little soul. (*She wipes her eyes, then her nose, with her hand, then becomes brisk again.*) Here—come on. We'll edge in a bit further, an' then 'ave a bite o' victuals.

(*She goes off* R., *followed by the others.*)

(*Off; protesting.*) All right, *all* right! If 'twas your foot, I've as much right 'ere as anybody else, 'aven't I? 'Tis a poor job if a free Englishwoman can't 'ave a few rights an' privileges.

(*Sad music fades in. The sound of hammering grows louder and continues into the next scene.*)

SCENE 3

SCENE.—*An upper room in the house of Nathaniel Partridge, on Tower Green. Just before ten o'clock on the same morning.*

The only entrance is across the R. *corner, up stage, but is narrower than in the anteroom setting. A small window, set in a thickness of wall, is up* L., *with steps leading up to it. There is a table up* C. *with a chair above it so that the user faces straight down stage. On the table are inkstand, quills, sand-sprinkler and paper, also a prayer-book. Down stage* L. *is a stool.*

(*See the Ground Plan at the end of the Play.*)

When the CURTAIN *rises, morning light through the window lights up the table and the corner of the room up* L. JANE *is seated at the table, writing. She wears the white or light dress which she wore in Act I, Scene 1. For a moment she writes, calmly.*

JANE (*reading as she writes the last words*). "Your obedient daughter till death, Jane Dudley."

(*She sprinkles sand on the letter, shakes it, folds and addresses it. As she is doing so,* ELLEN *enters. She is dressed in black, and is controlling her grief by a very great effort. She moves to* R. *of the table.*)

I have been writing to my father. He must be in sad case. He will blame himself for my death.

ELLEN (*with difficulty*). And so he should! Marring all by that insane rebellion . . . (*She breaks off.*)

JANE. He must not blame himself. For once in his life he may have acted to help me. Do you know when he is to die?

ELLEN. No, my Lady.

JANE. Has—mother visited him?

ELLEN. Not she. She has forsaken him as she has forsaken you.

JANE. Ah! Poor father! May he be given strength.

ELLEN. There is another matter . . . (*She hesitates.*)

JANE. Yes, Ellen?

ELLEN. A message from your husband.

(JANE *stiffens.*)

He craves a last moment with you. The Queen has consented to it.

(*The hammering stops.*)

JANE. I cannot see him.

ELLEN. But, child—to see him now—to say farewell . . .

JANE. No, Ellen. I am prepared, and so, I hope, is he.

ELLEN. If it would strengthen him . . .

JANE (*rising, interrupting*). It would not. If he is not strong already, I cannot strengthen him with my eyes nor my words. Let our next meeting be in a better world, where there are no misunderstandings.

ELLEN. Very well, my Lady. I will tell them so.

JANE. He goes—before I do?

ELLEN. Yes, child.

JANE. Let them tell him I will watch from this window as he goes, and wave to him.

(ELLEN *turns, and exits* R. JANE *stands for a moment in deep thought, then she moves down to the stool and kneels on the floor, using the stool as a prie-dieu. She puts her hands together and prays.*)

O merciful God, be Thou now unto us a strong tower of defence, I humbly entreat Thee. Give us grace patiently to bear what is to come: nothing doubting or mistrusting Thy goodness towards us: for Thou knowest what is good for us better than we do. Therefore do with us in all things what Thou wilt; only arm us, I beseech Thee, with Thine armour, that we may stand fast. (*She remains for a moment as if continuing silently.*) I am assuredly persuaded that all Thou doest cannot be but well; and unto Thee be all honour and glory—Amen.*

(*She remains kneeling for a moment longer. Drums are heard off* L. JANE *rises and goes to the window, standing there, looking off.* ELLEN *enters and stands* R., *watching her anxiously. The drums grow louder. Footsteps are heard in a slow march.* JANE *catches her breath on a sob and for a moment leans back against the wall.* ELLEN *moves quickly to her.* JANE *controls herself and leans forward, waving her handkerchief from the window, smiling. The drums are very loud beneath the window, then the sounds begin to fade away.* JANE *turns suddenly and buries her face in* ELLEN'S *shoulder.* ELLEN *puts her arms about her. The sounds die away in the distance.* JANE *draws away from* ELLEN.)

ELLEN. It is time to change your dress, child.

(JANE *moves down to the stool and sits on it.* ELLEN *goes off, to return in a moment with the black and white dress and head-dress worn by* JANE *in the Prologue, also a hand mirror. She places the head-dress and mirror on the table, and the dress over the chair, which she moves below the table.* JANE *rises.* ELLEN *moves to her and undoes her white dress.*)

JANE (*during this*). Do you remember the lily-pool at Bradgate? I fell into it when I was little—do you remember?—all among the red carp.

ELLEN (*busy with fastenings*). I remember. You were nearly drowned.

JANE. Yes. (*Pause.*) But I was not meant to drown.

(ELLEN *buries her face for a moment in the folds of* JANE'S *dress, then controls herself and takes it off.*)

They say, Ellen, that a traveller might go twelve miles, on a summer day, through the great woods around Bradgate, and never see the sun.

ELLEN. I would we were there now.

---

* Adapted from a prayer actually written by Lady Jane Grey while a prisoner in the Tower.

JANE. It is God's will that we should be here.

ELLEN (*suddenly passionate*). God's will that you should be here, in this case? You—a child, and innocent? No, I'll not believe it! (*She bursts into tears.*) I'll not believe it—if I am to believe in God.

JANE (*shocked*). Hush, Ellen! (*More gently, putting her arms about* ELLEN.) Dear Ellen! (*They stand so for a moment, then* JANE *gently pushes* ELLEN *away.*) My dress.

(ELLEN *controls herself, takes the white dress and lays it across the chair, removing the black and white dress. She is dressing* JANE *in this when the drums are heard again.* JANE *stiffens in sudden horror, breaks from* ELLEN *who would restrain her, and moves quickly to the window.*)

ELLEN. No, no! Don't look out now! They're bringing his body back.

JANE. I must look.

(*Clutching her half-fastened dress around her, she looks from the window. She is horrified, but steeling herself to watch. The drums and marching feet grow louder.*)

Guildford! Guildford! Ah!

(*She puts her hands to her face and falls back into* ELLEN'S *arms.* ELLEN *supports her to the chair, throwing the white dress on to the floor.* JANE *lies back in the chair, fainting.* ELLEN *chafes her hands. The drums and marching feet die away. A bell begins to toll, and continues to the end of the play.*)

ELLEN. I would you need never wake from this.

(*After a moment or two* JANE *revives. She smiles weakly at* ELLEN.)

JANE. I am—less strong—than I thought.

ELLEN. Be still, child. Rest.

JANE. I am—well—now. (*She pauses. Fearfully.*) Will it hurt, Ellen?

ELLEN. No, my dear.

(JANE *clings to* ELLEN *for a moment longer, then rises.* ELLEN *pulls herself together and completes the fastening of the dress. Then she arranges* JANE'S *hair, puts on the head-dress, and holds up the mirror for* JANE *to see herself.*)

JANE. Is it nearly time?
ELLEN. Yes.

(JANE *goes to the table and takes up her prayer-book and opens it. She stands* C., *facing down stage. Drums and slow-marching feet are heard off* R. *They grow loud and stop, apparently just outside the entrance.*)

JANE. I must have more courage. There is a time to be born, and—a time to die.

(*She turns and goes off, quietly, followed by* ELLEN. *There is a brief pause, during which only the tolling bell is heard. The room is empty, with* JANE'S *white dress lying on the floor. Then the drums and marching feet begin again. These again fade away, and once more only the bell is heard.*)

CURTAIN.

FURNITURE AND PROPERTY PLOT.

PROLOGUE

Off R.
    Scroll for HERALD.
    Prayer-book for JANE.
    Axe for EXECUTIONER.

Off L.
    Crown, sceptre and orb for EDWARD.
    Rosary and crucifix for MARY (to be worn throughout play).
    Book for JANE.

Effects.
    Opening music.
    Funeral bell.
    Roll of drums.
    Virginals record (or piano music).

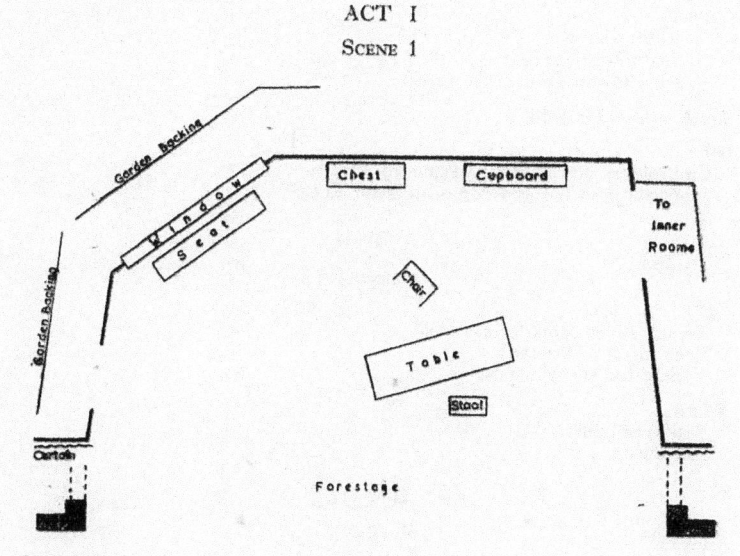

ACT I

SCENE 1

[Stage diagram: Garden Backing at left and upper-left; Window Seat along upper-left wall; Chest and Cupboard along back wall; exit "To Inner Rooms" at right; Chair, Table and Stool centre; Curtain at lower left and lower right; Forestage at front.]

On Stage.
    Refectory table. *On it :* vase of July flowers, pair of man's riding-boots.
    Cupboard or sideboard. *On it :* large jug of ale and two or three tankards.
    Window-seat with cushions.
    Small chest or table. *On it :* vase of July flowers.
    Chair.
    Stool.
    Vase of July flowers on window-sill.

Off R.—Riding-boots (as thrown from stage) for ELIZABETH.

Off L.—Duster for KATE.

Effects.—Virginals (continued from Prologue).

ACT I

Scene 2

Off R.
  Basket for 1st WOMAN.
  Duck or rabbit for 2nd WOMAN.
  Two sticks for 3rd WOMAN.

Effects.
  Galloping hooves.
  Music.

ACT I

Scene 3

On Stage.
  Furniture as Act I, Scene 1.
  May flowers in the three vases.

  Strike.
    Riding-boots.
    Jug and tankards.
    July flowers from three vases.

Off R.—Book for JANE.

Off L.
  Embroidery for NORTHUMBERLAND.
  Light summer hat and cup of milk for ELLEN.

ACT II

Scene 1

Off L.
  5 small silver coins for 1st WOMAN.
  Rose for 2nd WOMAN.
  2 sticks for 3rd WOMAN.

Effects.
  Peal(s) of bells.
  Sad music.

ACT II

Scene 2

On Stage.
  Furniture as Act I, Scene 3.
  July flowers re-arranged in the three vases.
  Bowl of fruit on the table.
  Sheathed sword on the chest.
  Open book on the floor near the window.
  Strike.—May flowers from three vases.

Off L.
  2 candelabra with candles for KATE.
  Lighted taper for KATE.
  Tray with vessel of wine and several goblets (only one to be used) for RICHARD.
  Letter for RICHARD.

Effects.—Knocking on door L.

ACT II
Scene 3

Off L.
> 2 large leather tankards for 1st WOMAN.
> 2 small stools for 2nd WOMAN.
> 2 sticks for 3rd WOMAN.

Effects.
> Funeral bell.
> Buzz of voices, off L.
> Shouting, off L.
> Peal(s) of bells.

ACT II
Scene 4

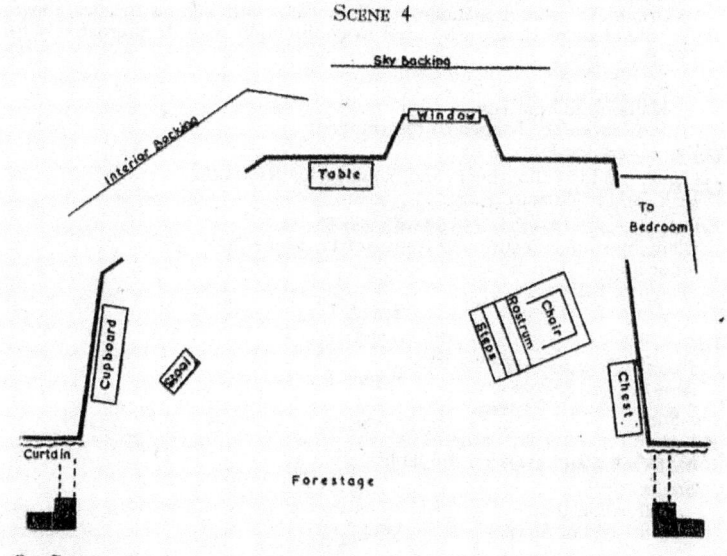

On Stage.
> Chair of state with canopy (as described in text). (Alternatively, ordinary carved high-backed armchair.)
> Rostrum (in two sections) to lift chair by two or three steps.
> Refectory table. *On it :* large vase ; pile of July flowers and branches.
> Small chest or table. *On it :* vase of flowers as above.
> Cupboard.
> Stool.
> Halberd.

Off R.
> Pattens for JANE.
> Crown, on crimson or purple cushion, for SUFFOLK.

Off L.—Slippers for KATE.

Effects.—Peal(s) of bells.

ACT II

SCENE 5

Off R.—Royal standard and naked sword for OFFICER.

Effects.
    Fanfare.
    Voices.
    Drums.
    Clanging sounds (as described in text).

ACT II

SCENE 6

On Stage.
    Furniture as Act II, Scene 4.
    Candelabra with lighted candles on the table, cupboard and chest.
        (Optional: a large standard candelabrum with lighted candles above the chair of state, to be used in conjunction with or alternatively to the above.)

Strike.
    Halberd and pattens.
    Flowers to be changed or re-arranged.

Off R.
    Cloak, muddy riding-boots and bandage for RICHARD.
    Fish for 1ST WOMAN.

Effects.
    Clanging sounds (continued from Act II, Scene 5).
    Knocking on door R.
    Peal(s) of bells.

ACT III

SCENE 1

On Stage.
    Furniture as Act II, Scene 6.
    MARY's hat and cloak on the table.

Strike.
    All candelabra.
    All vases of flowers.

Off R.
    Inventory for MARY.
    Miniature for MARY.
    Ring for MARY.

ACT III

SCENE 2

Off L.
    Basket for 1ST WOMAN.
    2 sticks for 3RD WOMAN.

Effects.
    Hammering on wood.
    Sad music.

ACT III
Scene 3

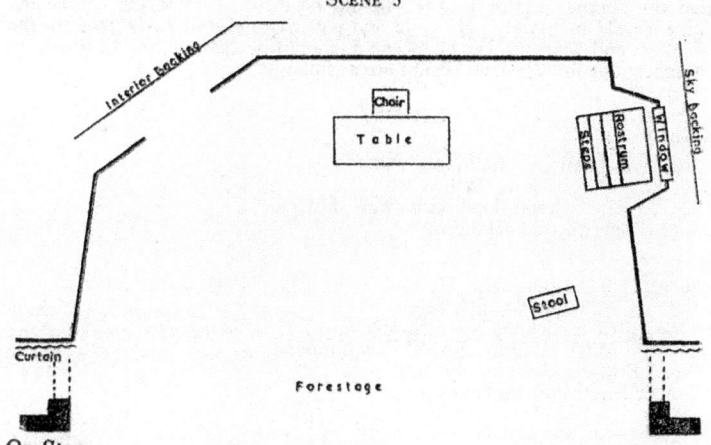

On Stage.

  Refectory table. *On it :* inkstand with quills, sand sprinkler, paper, prayer-book.
  Chair.
  Stool.
  Steps to window (being front part of the rostrum from Act II, Scene 4).
  Handkerchief for JANE.

Off R.

  Black and white dress and head-dress for JANE.
  Hand mirror.

Effects.

  Hammering on wood (continued from Act III, Scene 2).
  Drums (off L.).
  Slow-marching feet (off L.).
  Drums (off R.).
  Slow-marching feet (off R.).
  Bell.

NOTE.—A conventional design of Tudor roses, heraldic shields, banners, tapestries and/or painted cloths may be used at pleasure in various ways to enliven a curtain setting.

LIGHTING PLOT.

For the PROLOGUE and the interlude scenes on the forestage, the floats should be used, coloured and controlled as desired by the producer. Spots, from the perches and/or F.O.H., should be directed on to the characters. These should be mainly pale Gold and pale Salmon, but Lady Jane, in the Prologue, and Mary in Act II, Scene 5, should be spotted No. 17 Steel.

Suggestions for the main scenes are as follows :—

ACT I

SCENE 1

Floats and battens, all circuits, full.
Flood garden backing, White, frost.
No. 53 pale Salmon flood on backing down R.
Amber lengths on backing up L.

SCENE 3

Floats, No. 18 Blue, No. 51 Gold, at $\frac{1}{2}$. No. 7 Pink, $\frac{3}{4}$.
Battens, all above circuits, full.
Flood garden backing No. 3 Straw.
Flood through window, No. 53 Pale Salmon.
No. 3 Straw on backing down R.
Amber lengths on backing up L.

ACT II

SCENE 2

Floats, No. 18 Blue, No. 51 Gold, at $\frac{1}{2}$.
No. 1 Batten, No. 18 Blue, No. 51 Gold, at $\frac{3}{4}$.
When candelabra are lighted : No. 51 Gold pools on and around table, chair and stool. At the same time, bring up Gold in battens by $\frac{1}{4}$, and add Pink $\frac{1}{4}$, to floats and battens.
Flood on garden backing, No. 17 Steel, double.
Flood through window, No. 17 Steel and medium frost.
Blue and Amber on backing downstage, R.
No. 8 Salmon added to Amber on backing up L.

SCENE 4

Floats, No. 18 Blue, No. 51 Gold, No. 7 Pink, at $\frac{3}{3}$.
No. 1 Batten, ditto, at $\frac{3}{4}$. Other battens, at $\frac{1}{2}$.
No. 53 Salmon flood through window, directed towards down R.
Spots, No. 51 Gold, from bar or perch, at O.P., on dais and chair.
Ditto, No. 53 Salmon, from P.S., on R.C. acting area.
No. 51 Gold on backing up R. No. 4 Amber on backing up L.

SCENE 6

Floats, No. 18 Blue, $\frac{1}{2}$. No 51 Gold, $\frac{1}{4}$.
No. 1 Batten, No. 18 Blue, $\frac{3}{4}$, No. 51 Gold, $\frac{1}{2}$.
No. 51 Gold spots on acting areas—dais and chair, stool, table, court cupboard, etc., appropriate to candelabra.
Flood on exterior backing, combined No. 40 Blue and No. 3 Straw.
No. 17 Steel, double, on backing R. No. 8 Salmon on backing L.

ACT III

SCENE 1

Floats, No. 18 Blue, No. 51 Gold, at $\frac{3}{4}$.
Battens, No. 18 Blue, No. 51 Gold, full.
O.P. perch : No. 53 Pale Salmon on dais and chair.
P.S. perch : No. 53 Pale Salmon on stool, R.C.
Flood exterior backing No. 17 Steel and frost.
No. 51 Gold on backing R. Amber lengths on backing L.

Scene 3

Floats, No. 18 Blue, No. 51 Gold, ¾.
No. 1 Batten, No. 18 Blue, No. 51 Gold, full.
Other battens, ditto, at ½.
Perches or F.O.H. flood table and C. area, No. 53 Pale Salmon.
No. 51 Gold on backing R.   No. 18 Blue on exterior backing L.
Flood through window and across table, No. 17 Steel and frost.

PLAYS
by T. B. MORRIS

In Three Acts
(or equivalent)

THE ARROW OF SONG
THE BEAUTIFUL ONE
JOHN BULL'S ROUNDABOUT
MURDER WITHOUT MEN
THE SONG OF ENGLAND
THAT STATE OF LIFE

In One Act

BACKGROUND FOR TRAGEDY
CARNIVAL OF STEEL
CASSANDRA
CATS OF EGYPT
THE CUSTOMER IS ALWAYS RIGHT
THE FIELDS OF BETHLEHEM
GILD THE MASK AGAIN
GOSSIP'S GLORY
LION OF SPARTA
THE LITTLE NUT TREE
MADEMOISELLE DEPARTS
A MAN IN A STREET
MIRROR TO ELIZABETH
NIGHT ON THE HILL
OPHELIA
ORANGES AND LEMONS
PETTICOATS PREFERRED
THE PRISON ACROSS THE STREET
PROGRESS TO FOTHERINGHAY
RENAISSANCE NIGHT
THE SCARLET PEST
THE SHADOW OF A QUEEN
SHALL WE LEAVE THE GENTLEMEN
THE SPANISH LADY
SWAN-SONG
THE TRIAL OF HELEN
TUDOR THORNS
TWO AUNTS AND A GRANDMOTHER
TWO LADIES OF FLORENCE
UNTO WHICH IT SHALL PLEASE GOD ...
THE VOICE OF THE PEOPLE
WHITE QUEEN, RED QUEEN
WILD FOR TO HOLD
THE WILFUL WIFE
THE WOMAN

Children's Plays

SLEEPING BEAUTY
THE TRUTH ABOUT THE TARTS

Mock Trial

SIMPLE JUSTICE

In Volumes

AS ONE WOMAN TO ANOTHER, containing " As One Woman to Another ", " Fame ", " Whipped Cream in Sèvres ".
FOR A WOMAN OR TWO, containing " Taking it Both Ways ", " One of the Only Ways " and Five Monologues for Women.

SAMUEL FRENCH LIMITED